Last Stanza Poetry Journal

Issue #11: The Outsider

Edited by Jenny Kalahar

Stackfreed
Press

Illustrations other than those by LindaAnn LoSchiavo and Bill Traylor are by anonymous outsider artists.

"Afternoon in Marrakech" by James Green was previously published in *Ode to El Camino de Santiago and Other Poems of Journey* (Wipf and Stock, 2022).

"Snake" by Cynthia T. Hahn was first published in *The Ekphrastic Review*.

A previous version of Lois Baer Barr's Bill Traylor poem appeared in *The Ekphrastic Review*.

Kathryn Dohrmann's "Untitled (Man, Woman), ca. 1940–1942" was first published in *The Ekphrastic Review*.

A previous version of Michael H. Brownstein's "The Bad Luck Child" was published in *Dime Show Review*.

The illustration accompanying "Mango Selling in Manhattan is Dangerous" is by the poet LindaAnn LoSchiavo.

The interview with Hiromi Yoshida contains an excerpt from her "Icarus Burning." It originally appeared in *Bathtub Gin* #11 (Fall/Winter 2002) and was reprinted in: *Icarus Burning* (Finishing Line Press, 2020).

Eleanor Roosevelt by the Roadside

My dad's cousin, out for a spin, once saw
her leaning against the car, door open,
casually reading a map, and offered to help.
It wasn't far from Hyde Park, sunlight
unspooling through trees turning coppery,
fall crisp in the air. But she knew where
she was, she said, smiling—well, she had a way
about her, didn't she? Self-assured, yet
like your old neighbor in Saturday clothes.

Elsewhere, Jews waited for a knock, hunkered
in cellars and barns, grew lice. Packed trains
chuffed along the tracks, children clutching
their mothers' empty breasts. Every day
the smoke-filled air puffed them to oblivion.

History's full of "what-ifs"—a hoped-for détente,
a secret mission or plan hatched at night
over coffee and brandy, cicadas ratcheting up
their nocturnal buzz. Well, she would have
defied the president, wouldn't she? Made
her own deals with those to whom it mattered,
steeled by her urgency, her ruthless drive,
that iron-gray hair escaping its plain wire pins.

What had she come from, or where was she
going alone on a late summer day? Somewhere,
the death toll climbed into millions, chimneys
belched, gunfire rang out, sharp in the autumn
chill. Somewhere, the long negotiations
dragged, stalled, ended as footnotes.

The weather was very fine. They stood
there a moment, curious, friendly, fields
gold and green spread before them.
But there was nothing more to say.
When she was done, she folded
her map resolutely and drove away.

Diane G. Scholl

Norway, 1930

They ate fresh shrimp from newspaper
cones, skating on the pavement by
the old, green-spired church, which wasn't
allowed. Warm afternoons they snuck
away to swim, forbidden by their timid
Bestemor, two brothers lost at sea.

Nights the traded guilt, recriminations
in Norwegian rolled over their heads
like waves, the stormy tears. Days
they played on the rocks, fought,
helped Bestefar clean the stable, new
words washing their salty tongues.

On the way home they were seasick again.

They never went back, Dad and his brother:
the Depression, night school, war closing
like a fist, Norway in the lobster pot
of deep austerity. In Brooklyn, their mother
opened thin blue airmail letters, blotted,
terse, censored, and worried herself to fitful
sleep. They studied engineering, rode
the subway in a cloud of impersonal noise,
pretended they knew only English.

Sometimes they recalled the other side,
borrowed skates circling, that first plunge
into dark depths—a second baptism—
the ocean's raw, wild taste.

They might have dreamed the model ship
suspended on wire in the nave's long aisle,
sailing motes of dust, poised between
two worlds but never reaching port.

Diane G. Scholl

2

Say Her Asian Name

Since her arrival in the United States of America,
her Chinese name (whatever it had
been) blurred away—a smudged sequence of ink-
        brushed ideographs,
signifying sounds butchered by tripping, Anglicizing
tongues, lopped into bite-
sized *ching-chong* onomatopoeia,
off-key singsong syllables (two

Zen hands clapping). She was
the Atlanta gunman's pathological
symptom, his sin,
massage parlor whore,
Orientalized desire victim,
paper China doll tucked

away into stale fortune cookies
incinerated after the spark of
candlelight vigils
in March 2021 ignited #StopAsianHate
hashtags, and her papery

edges caught fire—the Asian
American dream gunned
down (no mountains of gold)—Chinatowns
        oozing away—eliding glossy tourist pamphlets,
sticky with chop suey fingerprints.
Even now, she has no real (Chinese) name

(Maxine Hong Kingston's "no-
name woman"), the spectral signifier rising from

phoenix ash. So, say her Asian name (her no-name
woman's name): Xiaojie ("Emily") Tan,

3

"Xiaojie," a Mandarin prefix and slang
for "prostitute;" "Emily," a whitewashing
(parenthetical) afterthought—she is the ideograph slipping away
toward the lexicography of new

              hashtags, that smudgy marginal gloss
(drop of coagulated vigil candlewax)
—paper money burning for the unappeasable gods
squatting on gold mountains.

Hiromi Yoshida

Soundings

In Didsbury village, birdsong
        is different. Not the dawn Chicago chatter
                of hapless sparrows nesting in skyscraper eaves.

Not the New York pigeons
        wobbling among park benches, foraging for crumbs,
                or giant robins of suburbia
        diving the shrubs with noisy wings
                defending their blue-egg nests.

Here,
        English finches chirp
                from tiled rooftops, their random salutations
                        veiling a rain-drenched sky. In the mornings,

the lark's clear melody cloaks the sunrise
                in hymnody, and at vespers,
        the nightingale's echo
                        rides the evening chimney to chimney,
                the hum of its elegy settling on the rushes.

The vagaries of wind
        chase swifts
                flitting along the canal, darting
                        among pubs and barns into
        a violet sky.

Donna Pucciani

Flat

I have spent a lifetime
far from the mountains.
I had to make a living.
It's the dark huddle of hills
I miss, their wall of orange in October,
the empty, smoking mines
carved from the full-bellied earth.
One day in college, walking
to an early-morning class,
I remember ash falling like rain
from a ruined mound of coal,
a mouth still chewing wads of black.
In the steep, slanted towns,
big Victorian houses were cheap,
built on ground that could collapse
at any time, perfect for professors
who invited students for cheer and metaphor.
Now I try gratitude
for decades of gainful employment
without a view of those hills. I have learned
to appreciate flat golden fields
meeting a straight edge of blue,
the great bland emptiness.
But other times I miss
the sweet claustrophobia
of youth, waking to dark mountains,
a slim thread of sky
winding up my ball of dreams.

Donna Pucciani

Inside, but Out

[Freshman Dorm, 1970]

What happened to the girl who
painted her whole face
in geometric sections like a fake Picasso in a dentist's office
and stormed into the dormitory lounge
shouting
that she didn't want to recognize herself?

What happened to the girl who,
funny and good-natured in the daylight,
grew agitated every evening
until she'd made a bedroll
to carry with her into the darkness
of a nearby church to cower,
curled between pews to hide and sleep?

What happened to the girl who
couldn't wake each day
except to sometimes eat one meal
but sprawled instead inside her room,
 unconscious on a mound of garbage
—food wrappers, rolling papers, soiled plates, and filthy laundry—
that spilled out from her bed and reached the door?

What happened to the girl who
roamed the hallways naked,
refusing to dress,
and smuggled in a snappish, un-housebroken wire-haired fox terrier
who shed families of fleas across the building's carpets
and up and down her own unshaven legs?

What happened to the girl who
moved a man—
released from jail after unspecified offenses—
into her double room
and whispered dialogue from therapy
("As long as we're both honest …")
just ten feet from her wide-eyed roommate's bed?

What happened to that *other* girl,
the one who'd fled her high school early,
eager to begin life as a Poet
(a word that always started with a capital)
and write her poems every morning at a college
that said it welcomed freedom and free spirits?
You know, that *other* girl who
stopped
—bewildered, baffled, and then horrified—
and gave up writing anything
for half a century
until confronting memories like these,
the fading image
of a generation
of those outside and left outside—
of wasted, damaged
girls.

Margaret D. Stetz

A Woman's Journey

Never left home, they said,
but she traveled beyond
deep down where internal
difference inheres. Her soul

selected her own society; she
knew she need not be a large
chamber to be haunted. She rode
that certain slant of light which

flashes us into worlds
that science can't measure.
She knew this world is not
Conclusion, and explored another,

took the route of evanescence
and soared on whirring wings
of hummingbirds that delivered
her to a Tunisia in the mind.

She had no time to stop for death
because she was always descending
into and beyond herself to taste a liquor
never brewed, telling all the dark

truth but telling it slant, writing
letters to a world that never
wrote back, staring into mysteries
that pervade wells, growing

accustomed to the dark. She
kept the Sabbath by looking
at creatures outside her self,
ecstatic to hear an oriole sing

but unsure of the source of
the song or what it signified,
certain only that success
is counted sweetest by those

who never succeed. She lived
and died for beauty but was
reborn into the glorious gift
of being able to make a prairie

with just one clover and one
single solitary-but-potent bee.
She dwelt eternally in possibility.
Her carriage held Immortality.

Norbert Krapf

Home Alone

All along she went
to church at home alone,
in the garden, in the orchard,

composing her skeptic's prayer
even as she took off from
her parents' property

by descending into darkness
no other rider of words
would dare confront.

The iconoclast daughter
encountered worlds at every
plunge, going down deeper

into rungs of consciousness
& shadowy continents where
no explorer had ever gone.

Silently, she pulled back up
into kitchen light where
she baked daily bread

sharing with almost no one
her raids on the eternal interior
except the sister who found her

red-hot words scrawled onto folded
sheets of paper stitched together,
left behind for someone to find.

Norbert Krapf

Camp Loneliness

If loneliness starts to eat
away at your empty insides

step outside of yourself
and look for the same

kind of image you see
in the mirror, on the face

of another human being.
Say hello in the way you

like hearing it said to you.
Then go off as a team of two,

split apart, and each search
for that look on another face.

All four of you come back,
build and light a fire, tell

one another your names,
and explain why you're lonesome.

Make use of stories to do so.
Tell those stories to one another

when the woods are darkest
and the fire burns brightest.

Others will come out of the dark to
listen. Fires and stories spread fast.

Somebody make notes and take turns
writing down your stories as best

you can. Turn those stories
into poems, songs, or prose

and invite more to the fire.
Share the wealth of your loneliness.

Pitch tents in a circle around
the embers of the fire. Wake up

when the sun rises and boil eggs
in a pot. Eat them with a little

salt if you can find any. Give
a name to the site where you

have shared your loneliness stories.
Give one another new names if you

forgot the ones you once had.
Give one another the gift

of wide-open ears and a voice
that says "Yes, but tell me more."

Always leave or make space for sturdy
tents to shelter new storytellers to come.

                                        Norbert Krapf

Biome

I am in a plastic bubble
on a hill in Northern Europe,
in a habitat created to display
another biome. My biome.
I walk past the spines
of my favourite cactus
and squeeze the plump fingers
of the succulent plants.
The sharp sage of high chaparral
tickles my nose. This is
where I came from, an arid place
not without beauty.

I remember breaking off the aloe vera
leaf to rub into a burn.
I remember gently separating the prickly pear
cactus into separate pots.
I remember waiting for the vivid bloom
of my unwelcoming friends.

I cannot connect with the trees
outside this dome, so tall and
green with names I do not know.
How did this become my home?
All damp and often dark,
these trunks are carpeted with moss,
the soil moist and fecund.

But sometimes,
I long for sand
and spines
and rattlesnakes.

Frances Gaudiano

The Salt Taster

Fresh water floats on
the surface, salt sinks.
Even a sip fatal to rice fields.
The tide rises up a river
toward someone else's boy.
Again and again, he dips
his black head, sips,
silent, rootbound,
as tight as the small plant
he is, angel-wrapped, he dips
and sips, tasting the water.
Slight trembles. Dips and sips,
searching the end of the sluice
for the first sign of salt.

Michael Ansara

A Moment with Swans

I broke the bread of condolence,
solemnly offered it to the waters,
a pool of gathered tears,
shiny glass shattered by a loss
rippling though our lives,
a circle growing—
calling to an approaching lamentation,
trumpets muted,
who take our offerings and water,
feeding upon our sorrows.

I fear the pond
will never be the same,
the shore forever changed
by the churning of emotion
that washes up in waves
through the reeds and grasses
until we all will grow still.

Michael E. Strosahl

Ghyu Means Love in Nepali
~ *after Mansi Dahal*

We have so few words for love in this language much of the world seems to prefer. What is the word for when love freezes? The word for a love that hesitates? Burns? Crashes? In English, love needs adjectives and metaphors—it can't stand on its own. I'm told that snow in Inuktitut has many words, and I wonder do they also parse the notion of loving with the same precision? Such as wet love, icy love, melting or fresh love, fragile love—the kind so thin it gives way under the slightest pressure. The Greeks have understood this need for distinction. Love for everyone is agape; sexual love is eros; philia for friendship; ludus for playful love; philautia for love of the self; storge for unconditional or familial love; and for a longstanding, committed, companionate love, pragma. Even the poets struggle, having to dress up their love in fancy clothing. For instance, a gauzy dress will suit translucent love. What kind of love wears a suit, a tutu? And what of naked love? It may take only a day or two for love to change its garb from a swirling chaos of reds and purples to something stripped down, maybe a nylon slip or a straitjacket. Some loves wear the same practical shirt and pants for decades. From garters to turtlenecks, from silk to synthetics, I've worn them all. All, that is, except the one the Greeks call pragma. If I could, I would detail its lines and its seams, the way the fabric moves when the beloved walks. I've been through my closets, and possibly yours as well, but not one pragma garment has ever fit me right.

Susan Wadds

Unbroken

There were times
I imagined you different.

My young mother mind
pictured you—
normal, typical, non-disabled.

I can't use those words anymore
for their opposites evoke—
lack, absence, tragedy,

and you, my child,
are a celebration of plenty,
a bounty of delight,
a well of fascination.

In fact, you stand against the backdrop
of pedestrian life
in sharp relief
adding color where there is none.

I looked up the opposite of disabled--
unaffected, activated, unbroken.

At twenty-nine, you appear much younger
and I wonder how typicality
would have changed you.

Plucked eyebrows,
black eyeliner,
a flat iron to tame
your wild dark chocolate curls?

You might have dieted,
finding fault with your shape and size,
and worn heels that hurt your tender feet.

You would not go singing
through the grocery store,
happily oblivious to strange looks.

Typical you
may not have sung at all,
thinking a note or two
off-key.

There are many times
I imagine the world
different than it is,
a welcoming place
where compassion and respect
are the norms,

and we all go singing
through the aisles.

Melinda Coppola

4:31

Let's say it's four thirty-one in the morning,

at any rate, before breakfast, when reverential
despair meets stolid determination, not at all

or not yet the confrontation of scalding oil

and scrambled egg, and yet something far more
disturbing, although the moon shines through it
and the sun doesn't bother to glare.

The dog would empathize if he could,
the cat says screw it; I've got fresher fish

that meets the eye. The uneasy agreement

between verb and cosmos is of little concern
to the cat, oh—and before I forget—

meet Henry, the cat in this picture,

who senses that in a couple of hours
the business news will try to fructify

and he'll have to shelve his aspirations,

save for several parceled treats,
until the planet delegates him
amanuensis. It's not as though

a clock is a manuscript you can
rely on, a town you can drive right by,

it's not a needle, sullenness

in its stop signs, no stoplight's red glare. Henry,
remember him, god love him, chooses not to care.

Bruce Robinson

22

Nuclear Winter

Is blood really thicker than water?
I wouldn't know.
I lost my only blood tribe years ago.
The family left to me is water only,
status conferred by decree, not blood,
and, by God, they show it.

I am the changeling, the stranger,
the foreigner, *der Ausländer,*
handed by pious venal hands
to a woman with the soul of a shopkeeper
and a man who didn't have the backbone
to gainsay her cruelties.

In a thousand ways, the lack of DNA is driven home—
first blamed, last praised, and used to it.
It might as well be on the town green
as an un-Wanted Poster.
But now I can laugh about it, sardonically,
while parading around in my black sheep coat.

There's no wool for anyone but me.
It's my only warmth; I have no master.
The old bitch dame can freeze, and the little boy
who lived down the lane is dead.
All hail the outlander, exiled to the barn—
she's tough enough to survive a nuclear winter.

RC deWinter

The Boy

c. 1919; Amedeo Modigliani; Italian, 1884-1920.

What is it, Boy? What is it?

Are you a Crown Prince Imp,
contemplating your next move?
There is no chessboard,
here, at this table, inside,
& so … are you simply bored?

Or are you an artistic dictator
        in the making?

        Are you an unfortunate Italian,
        being somewhere between
        ages 13 & 16
        in this year of your Lord
        now aged 1919?

Do you know what it is
of the World you will live?
Do you see Spain? Do you see Ethiopia?
Do you see Albania? Do you miss home?

Or do you know what you miss
        on this mirrored side
        of your pouting mouth
        or your squinting stare?

        Your face answers *No,*
        & does so politely enough.
        You show nothing less than
        a world's new weight
        on that slumped shoulder,
        & *this* question,
        flush-faced, firstly felt—
What is it?

J.T. Whitehead

Omen

Dragonflies dart, buzzing, zooming, cruising,
specks of red on green lakes and blue valley—
bad luck, Mama says, gardening,
sunhat drooping in the draping heat,
fake flowers as red as her blazing hair.
It's always an omen, something lurking,
black cats and shattered glass and butterflies.
(Her eyes dart like dragonflies
at every rustle or rattle or shadow.)

Is it now, says Papa,
staring down the dirt road. Is it now?
He chews on blades of grass,
on wood picks and carrot sticks,
constant as Mama's predictions.
He chews because if not he'll shout,
and he burned through too many sorrys by now.
(His head jerks up like a spooked horse,
like there's something spying, someone crying,
lights on all hours of the day.
Why? He won't ever say.)

Some guy waved at me today, says daughter.
She'll tuck her hand 'round her throat like a necklace,
like she knows it's time for slaughter.

Katherine Heil

Rainbow Man

The day after The Inauguration,
I went for a jog to the Hudson River
in the frigid early hours before the world
was up. Except, that is, for two strange legs—
strange, that is, in that I did not know them
as I knew most of the early morning crowd
of Pier 84—which I only saw
from behind, way out on the pier, above
the river, just across from the Intrepid
and the Concorde. The toes were pointing north,
toward George Washington, once a Founding Father
but now a Bridge. The feet filled two bright canvas
shoes with all the colors of the rainbow—
ROY G BIV—plus black and white. When I
jogged by, I could not see the face, but took
a chance and, to the jacket's back, I said,

> *You're walking on two rainbows. What I mean*
> *is that I get to walk on water, jog*
> *on water, every day, here on the pier,*
> *but you can say you're walking on rainbows.*

The rainbows turned to me and showed the face
of a young man. His skin was dark. And light.
He bore a single ring in his nose
like a genie or timeless avatar
or demigod, or some kid from the 'hood,
and beamed forth with a smile, making me glad
I took a chance on a stranger and spoke
(which is not always fortunate, alas).
And he said back to me, through the smile,
Thank you for that perspective. And I kept
jogging. A few laps later as he left
the pier and the park, he walked by and said,

Enjoy your day, which words might not have shattered
earth or shook the firmament, but in
the abracadabra way he beamed and walked
on rainbows, in a flash I felt I mattered
too.

James B. Nicola

One Epiphany in Six Movements

Christendom has abolished Christianity without really knowing itself. As a result, if something must be done, one must attempt to introduce Christianity into Christendom.
—Søren Kierkegaard

I. *Largo*

When Paddy saw the noose that day,
he suspected he had made a grave mistake
and had voted for the wrong person.
Hillary would not have summoned a lynch mob, he thought,
with the sight of the noose.
But this thought did not reach the front of his brain.
It was a thought he did not know he had. Yet.

II. *Adagio*

Then he saw the swastikas,
and since he was born without some toes and fingers and only one foot
(his mother suffering from German measles
in the months before he was born),
and since it had recently been impressed upon him that he,
a "differently-formed person,"
would have been one of the first incinerated
by the swastika-wielding Nazis,
that thought, that grave thought, started to move to the front of his brain,
to his mind, almost,
and he gasped at the sight of the swastikas.
He gasped but did not quite know why. Yet.

III. *Andante*

Then he saw the confederate battle flags,
not the national flag, the official flag, no, but rather the "stars & bars."
Both were symbols of treason, of lynching, of murdering
and getting away with murder—with murders, rather, a million or more—

28

but the battle flag was also incitement to violence:
of getting away with murder again today.

IV. *Moderato*

Then he saw their guns.
And with their guns, he saw and suddenly did not need to think
but knew what the mob—his mob, really, he thought—
had come prepared to do.
He knew when he saw the guns.

V. *Allegro*

And when the tally of the dead was tolled and death knells rung,
he could no longer think because he knew that his vote made him as well
a murderer.

VI. *Presto*

And now, with so much work to do and so little time to do it,
Paddy does a turnabout, decides not to murder anyone else,
decides to live as long as he can, to try his best to save a few lives
and maybe make up—though what can make up?—
for the dead whose assassins
his vote helped summon.
He decides to defy his wife at last, to ignore his petulant brother-in-law,
to give his life to country and God,
by living it all in service to both,
and secretly makes an appointment to get
the vaccine.

James B. Nicola

Middle Aged, Alone, and Working Through
One hundred Ways to Amuse Oneself.

Doloros had a head of curls dyed chocolate brown
and corkscrewed around a pale face rouged with Revlon
antique rose and perched on a slender neck attached

to a 16DD bust resting on a roll of soft never-lost baby fat dripping
over the always-tight waistbands of her always-long skirts *always*
spliced with a side split to give her legs freedom, she

said, to run and kick and dance the Charleston whenever the fancy
struck them, always un-stockinged and brown, and always crossed
when Doloros drank vodka from a champagne flute
sitting at her open window

naked from 5 pm on saturdays and sundays, never ever
on a weekday afternoon in case the neighbour's children
coming home from school got a fright and told their mothers who

would tell their fathers who would feel the rain coming and decide to
put the mower away until saturday or sunday when Doloros
would be sipping her vodka, slowly watching them watching her

the cat snuggled on her lap covering what her mother always called
her dignity, which Doloros thought was an odd thing to call
a shadowed place of nothing more than skin and hair
and perpetually dampened expectation

hidden under sensible and usually white cottontails
bought from Woolworths and always in a double pack.

Linda McQuarrie-Bowerman

First Sunday of Advent

Graying and gray couples scattered about the harsh-lit pews against black predawn windows. Celibate celebrant seeming somehow the happiest and most solemn. Wondering, perhaps, what these faithful will distill from their long marriages at this ritualized weekly reckoning. Wondering, one imagines, about their faithfulness. Well to the side and rear, meanwhile, their successors; slim sober pair juggling four kids under age five. Sex as utility and defense. As if to raise the odds against unhappy outcomes from the reckless foray of parenting. As if unaware of the infinite varieties of travail and bliss alike that fate, the gods, their God on the altar have at the ready. *Inshallah,* good Catholics. We are *Alive Together*, as the poet Lisel Mueller rhapsodized in her hymn to a random universe and its miracles. I hear again the voice of a perfectly improbable friend, reading those lines aloud to me and me alone, as I recite my rote prayers, and I allow wonder.

Dan Carpenter

Cat Burglar

An old moon, pale as honeycomb, lifts
    over the jumble of roofs, the sharp tilt of the chimneys,
    and escapes for a moment the racing clouds.
Below, it is a good night for a thief, and his step
    will go unnoticed under the scurrying wind.
It is one of the old professions,
    and he is good with his hands
    and knows things others don't, watches,
    observes the little habits of his neighbors,
    keeps a timetable, knows which doors are which,
    which windows they crack for air, knows
    that breeze, its restless sweeping of the brittle leaves,
    is his friend if he can stay in sync
    with its whimsical pulse, remain patient and alert.
A poet might learn a thing or two,
    hair-strung over such silence,
    treading lightly upon the eggshell paths,
    following the tiptoe shadows down deserted alleyways,
    slipping past and through and out
    of doors and windows, casements and cellars,
    inhabiting a sixth sense, studying
    the arcane craftsmanship
    of blades and locks, hairclips and gloves, ball bearings
    and the carefully measured placement of a dollop of oil.
If he can but anticipate the ending,
    uncover the jewels, the cash,
    the hidden heart of it all,
    and then find with his cold eyes that last step—
    dwell there, noiselessly, before his foot
    treads a fatal crease in the ancient floor—
    outfit himself this moment
    with a cloak finely woven as a poem,
    the theft and thief invisible under it,
    the perfect cloak within which to sail
    when all the sirens awake the night
    with the weary shock of their familiar song.

Marc Harshman

Defiant

A system of uncertainty has entered our daily life. The pressures of mechanization and uniformity to which it is subject call for protest and the artist has only one means of expressing this, by music. – Bohuslav Martinu

Mysterious freight rolled all afternoon through that wooden town between the two mountains. Below the tracks there were herons in the stream, snakes of fog rolling between their threadbare legs. Hana had been promised tea and cakes upon arrival, after which she was to wait for it to begin raining. She might have a long march ahead—there were many streets and even more alleys. Still, she had many songs inside her lonely head and sang them to herself as she worked the miles behind her.

Bohuslav Martinu had been sickly, born in a tower, carried one-hundred and forty-three steps daily by his father down, then up. Listen now to his flute slide down, then up, going somewhere. Hana would be going somewhere herself.

Speranza had risked poetry for her many lives. Her *fetch* had reached Reading Gaol from her deathbed in Chelsea. *If you are not too long, I will wait here for you all my life.*

Hana, though, wasn't to wait. The work found her, and to it she went. In the musty bedsit, she found she appreciated the old man guarding the stairs, who offered up his stories as if priceless ephemera. She would remember his trivia as a secret sacrifice and knew just the place for them in the filing cabinet with its coded pages, pages she'd marked with her magenta fingernails. Across that same room, in a corner, there was a small sofa on which she'd seen love clocked by the hour. There was a silk umbrella, too. Pink roses on a blood-red field.

Hana was young for espionage, but she carried it lightly: a flower in her hair, her back straight, her small breasts up, and a willingness to kiss strangers despite a lack of experience. A whiff of sex, and she'd all the gunpowder she needed. There were alleys made for innocent girls and lecherous men—were there any other kind? Their words fell out of the air and into her hands. Like *der vogelhändlerin*, she offered a bucolic disguise anyone would desire, and so she'd kept on offering what she didn't have, kept open every door in that slender forest of courtrooms and prisons, kept open every window that would sing her name. If the war went on long enough, she'd emerge with a pocket full of chances larger than the moon that slipped now from the clouds above that foggy stream. Herons were good luck. She counted them: one, two, three, *here,* and one, two, three, *there.* Almost like the waltz she danced last night with a man wearing a silver *totenkopf* on his black collar, his empty eyes following her every move. One. Two. Three. Almost like the measures to a waltz you might whistle mounting stairs in a lonely tower where poets breed and eternity comes close enough to believe, close enough if you are not too long in coming, to the kind of courage it took Hana to get there. Listen. She means to sing, to *express herself in music.*

Marc Harshman

Interior quotation attributed to Oscar Wilde, whose mother was the Irish poet, Speranza.

Tithonia

The tithonia I planted on the first day of August bloomed in the early morning of October 1. The sunburst petals arrayed around a yellow pistil the exact shade of spring. Along the five-foot stalk, another dozen blossoms swelled in their green cocoons. And I began to speak with this late prodigy. Of my deceased white German shepherd and of the songs I know by heart. "Ain't No Sunshine When She's Gone." "Crying Time." "One Headlight." Of the shipwrecks I survived on my voyage into being an American elder. All while the flower rested for its span against a late, but eager, winter. Offering its bouquet to the feeble sun of the tenth month. I weeded around the perimeter of the stalk, working manure into the soil. And cut back a thicket of honeysuckle to allow the noon sun a larger target from this fall surprise. Across the days and weeks, the Mexican sunflower unfurled its small autumn glories. And I shared stories of a 300-pound pig that flew nonstop on a jetliner from Philadelphia to Seattle and of a minor league catcher who tried to pick off a runner at third with an Idaho potato. I memorized "Brilliant Disguise" to serenade my garden's star for Halloween. In the mornings, I photographed the newest constellations with the sun at my back. To share with my friends who could hardly believe my luck during a time of rogue flurries and early freezes. In mid-November, I deadheaded a dozen of the spent flowers to let the seeds dry in a paper bag for a month. Afterward, it snowed every day in Indiana. Until I followed my footsteps across the white ground cover to where the leaves of the plant hung dark and ragged. And found myself unfamiliar with the requiem for a flower.

Michael Brockley

Boots

There's dirt on my sole, and my boots aren't zipped.
Some things I can change; some things I don't want to.
My unzipped boots connect me to my heart a world away.
The air smells different here.
Maybe I'm lost.

Put my heart in a jar and ferment me with cabbage.
I came to this place by choice, by privilege,
chasing a dream in unzipped boots.
Who am I here,
a world away from my heartbeat?
Temple dirt and ginkgo leaves
are a million miles beyond my red-dirt heart.

I tried to find myself,
but became lost.
I wasn't good at being home,
but I'm not good at being here, either.

And I'm not zipping my boots; you can stare all you want.
I want to be a ghost and drift,
unzipping skin to release my unsettled soul.
This road is like a leaf,
veins branching and reaching,
pulsing,
winnowing down to dirt on my soul
and unzipped boots.

Say Davenport

Temples

There are two kinds of temples in this town,
one of which doesn't even bother
to pretend.

The one kind I pass in the mornings,
watching acolytes in suits and ties
carefully stepping over a sleeping homeless person
while I put a handful of hieroglyphics in an old Starbucks cup—
rattling like a broken prayer wheel—
hieroglyphics that mean nothing
to anyone but humans.
The acolytes voraciously peek over,
and the hieroglyphics become real.

The other kind I pass in the evenings,
hearing a choir singing inside
shielded by walls thick as a fortress yet thin as paper
while I search my wallet for some spare change—
rattling like a broken prayer wheel—
to give to the homeless person
camping on the doorstep.
One more night.
In the form of a tiny silver moon.

There are two kinds of temples in this town,
to both of which I pay my tenth
for government-prescribed salvation,
and they all worship the same gods
even though they would furiously claim
otherwise.

Maximilian Speicher

When Morning Comes

At midnight, two am, three am, five,
the lights come on,
doors will be checked,
drawers opened and closed.
Maybe a bath will be taken
or a shower,
then twenty minutes later,
bags packed and unpacked.
Hunting for keys,
searching for a purse,
until a few hours of rest,
always with one eye open.

Breakfast is at one in the morning, three,
or whenever the urge is there,
but then forget that we ever had breakfast,
and forget that we ever slept,
and become frenzied
because we were supposed to be
on a train. We can't remember
the destination, but know that
we were supposed to leave.
Our agitation mounts
because we need to catch the train
or get into the car and go
somewhere, anywhere.

Then we try the lunch ritual,
but today, it does not work
because the food is poisoned,
or the food was stolen.
Or it needs to be taken back
to the children, but we can't
remember which children.

We pace back and forth through the house,
looking for people who have died,
but we know they must still be here.
"How dare you tell me that you think they've died,
that you haven't seen them? They were just here!"

At midnight or three or five,
we will start all over again,
fighting hard to recall
all that we have lost along the way
when morning comes.

RM Yager

Outsider at Dachau

The polite driver gestured
from the open door
   and invited tourists to enter:
"The bus is ready to leave."
I boarded with the burden
  of seeing
with a prolonged
     inattention to things—
  attempts to survive
as hopeless illness ravaged
where lies were the only truth.
I promised to remember,
  but lied,
hearing individual stories
  that once lived
inside the barracks floor,
    plans in well-swept order
leaving onlookers now
    to ask questions
they did not want
  answered
  in this carefully curated
     exhibition space—
the hunger, excrement, torture, blood
  erased.
The guards remain,
    like us, like me,
    as we were—
exiled from a humanity
  we had not thought of before.
    The bus is ready.
I thought it was a terrible crime
that would change us.
It is easier
  to visit a space
  than to visit a time,

not wanting
    to know more
as I turned away from
    the large gray
    metallic letters
that comment on forgetting—
  not forgetting, yet forgetting
the faces
  in the glassed-over
  collection of flat photos
that need to be
    looked at closer
before I leave them behind.
    The bus is ready.

Royal Rhodes

Inspection

Annoyed by a slow leak in a rear tire, I went to the service station today. Since I was already there, I got my truck inspected, although it didn't need doing for another month. In nearly fifty years of car ownership, this was the first time I was early with an inspection.

I am always, by design, at least a day or two late, which pushes the next deadline ahead two months. Long ago, it occurred to me that if I do this for six years running, I will save one year's inspection fee. The only caveat is that you need to bump into December and then February while the car is still relatively sound. Doing mandated repairs when snow is on the ground is a major-league pain in the ass.

My friend Larry, now long dead, once cut an ad from the Keene phone book yellow pages, one featuring the Old Man in the Mountain, and taped it to the top center of his windshield. He drove around southern New Hampshire for a couple of years with that counterfeit sticker, while from Vermont, I admired him fiercely.

It was Larry who gave me the wise advice that I should take my car to a garage run by fat older men because they were unlikely to get down on the ground to look for holes in the floorboards. Larry also sold me a $200 Saab that crumpled when I tried to jack it up to change a tire. Sharp fellow, that Larry.

When half my friends drove VWs, we would call around until we found four tires with decent tread, then get together and swap until one car had a complete set of inspectable tires. It would go off to the garage and get a sticker, and the tires would then go back to their various owners.

At Barton's Garage in Perkinsville, VT, I once waited to see if an aged VW bug would pass. It had a loose bumper mount on the rear, as was common with them, and I was hoping that the old fat guy theory would get me by this fatal defect. One younger man worked feverishly while two older ones sat beside the woodstove and talked. Eventually, one of the old guys got up and slowly, painfully walked around my sagging car and announced that it was okay. A minute or two later, the young man jumped into the front, scraped off the old sticker, and stuck on a new one. I paid him and got the hell out of there.

Also in my youth, before the day of aggressive glue and soft paper stickers, I could go to a junkyard in winter, find a recent wreck with a sticker that still had a few months on it, and pour hot water from a thermos onto a rag I held to the outside the windshield, over the sticker. As the glass expanded, the glue would yield, and I could watch the freed sticker float gently like a falling leaf to the dash. There was a simple beauty to its descent, which was as pleasant as scoring the free sticker.

I'm not sure what bothers me most about today's decision. I now have an October sticker, just like the one it replaces, instead of a December one which would have bought me two free months and headed me through the winter stickers before the truck got much older. I dutifully got my car checked when it was due, losing any pretense of outlaw status. Mostly, I fear that I have become one of those old fat guys, too lazy to do the job right.

Roderick Bates

Afternoon in Marrakech

Sunlight seeps through haze the afternoon
has collected, sinks onto canvas awnings

of *souks* at the edge of *Djemaa el-Fnaa*,
slips through tiny rents and casts

specks of light onto shadows
where women in hajibs, some in burkas,

sort produce into flat baskets, their fluid chatter
untethered to the work of hands.

A knot of men spills from a mosque then scatters,
some to the *souks*, a few to a *maqhaa* to games

of backgammon, the pieces all still in place,
and others disappear into a swarm of motorbikes.

One slaps the rear of a Vespa, yelling something
in jest to the driver, who turns and shouts a repartee.

A feral cat dodges the Vespa, raises its back and
struts to safety, curls around a post then

plops onto a spot of shade, flipping its tail
at anyone who noticed its brief loss of insouciance.

How familiar it feels to be the stranger,
to know the consolation of aloneness in a place

both alien and native, to see heat rise from cobblestones,
feel scorching air sink deep inside the lungs, and listen

to silent echoes of the call to prayer.

James Green

I can be whoever

you want me to be, maybe Susie,
and spend the night at your house,
but your mother will be annoyed
because we won't go to sleep.

We'll chatter and giggle and
both be twelve years old.
We'll sing all our favorite songs
from church and school.

You'll laugh telling me
how you like my older brother
and that I'm your very best friend.
But for me, that part

isn't pretending because we are
best friends, Mom, because
I've talked with you nearly every
day of my sixty years.

We've landed here with your worst fear.
You've forgotten that you have
a daughter; you don't know who
I am anymore. But I'll play pretend

so you can think you know me,
so I can watch your face erupt in quirky
smiles while you believe you're spending
time with your bestie by your side.

Marilyn J Baszczynski

Mom à la Modigliani

Don't be fooled by her frail appearance,
pencil-thin eyebrows, pale blue asymmetrical eyes,
rounded almonds that seem to look out a window
to reflect the sky, angular Cupid's-bow lips
tightly pursed as if impatient with the time
required to sit for an exercise in imitation.

I didn't see what the painter saw.
Despite his selective distortion—
slight tilt to elongated nose and neck—
the illusion of glamour drew me in
as a child, challenged me to find out
what made her tick, but she only offered
details on a need-to-know basis.

What did my father see? He painted her
wearing plain brown clothes she never
would have worn. Warm and safe, brown
softens flaws, draws attention elsewhere.

Who can tell her story? History told
by the young will differ from her tale.
I only know I would stare at the painting
that hung by her closet in our house in a city
divided by a river with hills all around.

Meg Freer

In and Out of the Rabbit Hole

for D.

You lost your dream
in a bottle, misplaced your will-
power in the promise to stop.

At some point, your scheme
to find happiness
broke into a thousand tiny pills.

There are too many stairs
to climb, not enough soup
in the bowl. There's no bit in the drill,

no wheel for the bike, no guest
for the long weekend of prayer.
God knows the truth, but he's not

telling us. We stand around
and watch you crawl back to square
one, barely able to hold your flesh

to the bone. If only there was a single shot
of hope, some crutches of inner peace,
a soothing cream of joy we could give you,

we could live with ourselves. But the knot
in your brain builds a nest
and the egg cracks, the lousy beast

walks into your house and you're
on the floor again, passed out.
Tomorrow, the sun will rise in the east.

May you wake up and stand in the light, finally blessed.

David James

Bill Traylor's "Brown House with Multiple Figures and Birds" (1939-1942)

may I write about this house?
those silhouettes, that ladder
men in stovepipe hats
dogs   foxes   giving chase
geese or vultures plunge and soar
away, away
shadows attack or surround
or flee
this empty house

Bill Traylor, born in Dallas County, Alabama
enslaved
freed from that house at twelve
to sharecrop
know Jim Crow and raise a family
live on Montgomery's streets

scavenge posters, scraps, boxes
to draw with pencil
then paint in his dotage
by the fruit stand or seated by the tavern

said he was born on April Fool's Day
but he was no fool
slept at the shoe store or the funeral home
when he could
or with a daughter
till he died October 1949
buried in an unmarked grave

I do not know the pain of living
where lynching
was common as cake walks
the stench and the stain
pain he numbed with drink
nor the joy Traylor felt at discovering paint
in his eighties

I need to stand in the graveyard
at Mount Mariah AME Zion
a tombstone marks the place
marks the span of one man
THROUGH HIS ART HE LIVES ON
Here, Traylor finally rests his bones

Lois Baer Barr

Snake, 1939-1942

Even the snake has room for complaint.
Wide mouth open to swallow, its still eye
spies us, judging our size, fangs bared.
It is black, and thin, and coiled but for a tail,
spiked as if testing the dull, orange air;
fissures sizzle around its head.
A famine sounding in a flat desert,
we stand accused and are stilled.

Cynthia T. Hahn

Inspired by Bill Traylor's work, "Snake"

Untitled (Man, Woman), ca. 1940-1942

art by Bill Traylor

Two fingers pointing,
Hello! Hello!
Like a cave painting
from Jim Crow,
a woman, a man,
tux and tall hat,
evening bag swinging
tick-tock on its chain.

Like a Rorschach
painted on cardboard.
So cool to strut
a finger dance.
So fierce to walk
a public spat.
Or maybe they're
jazzed-up Blues-ers
pointing to God.

Kathryn Dohrmann

Just send an email

With a link,
Faces like still clouds revolving in the eye

Invisible behind cybernetic walls.
Around us, breezes turn to gusts, knocking over antenna,

Spinning cars in concentric, horrifying circles: a Volkswagen,
Then a Toyota (the Fords don't lift, they only sulk and watch Fox News),

Collapsing whole towers in the miles-wide tornadic front,
Tourists flopping like the tuna before it was canned for their lunch,

A town of fishy, lifeless staring, screens switching sides,
A clicking sound following the terror of cyclic speech,

Faces making quieted gestures evermore still,
Pupils living a disbelief of hope.

Robert Simon

Lonely Town

The computer message board
keeps town residents informed
about more than village news,
weather, and traffic reports.
It also teems with lonely hearts.

"Hi everyone," one person wrote.
"I am no good at this.
I've been here almost 4 yrs
and made no friends.
It's been pretty rough.
Does anyone have time to text?"

Few did.
One person chided the writer
for not going to church.
"You can make friends there."
Another seemed to sympathize,
"I've been pretty much all alone
in this neighborhood myself."

Those two responses were the only ones on the first day.
It was apparent that the lonely heart would not respond,
not even when new texters reached out.
"You can message me if you need someone to chit-chat with."
Another wrote: "I understand how you are feeling.
It's a creepy empty feeling.
Would love to have a friend to laugh,
talk to, act crazy, and shed a few tears if needed."
Another wrote, "Life is crazy.
We chase what we can't have
and run away from what we desire the most."

Not all the responses offered a glimmer of hope.
"Hello! I've been here 35 years and no friends LOL!"

But it was the last response that intrigued me.
"I've been here for 5 years and only know a few local people.
I'm disabled and don't work.
I absolutely do not go to church (I'm atheopagan),
and being queer/polyamorous in a red state
means I get lots of judgment and very little acceptance.

Oh, yeah. I gotta write to this one.

David Allen

Imagining the Journey from Delhi

The whisper of a train
forms itself in my head

as if it is a memory
but is really an imagining

the click of tracks and smells
of a world full in my nostrils

and I am there while
against me an angular jut

of elbows and the left
wrist of humanity

leans into my waistline
hips on hips ankle bone

to ankle bone breathe in
breathe out the click pushes

through the electricity
of skin on skin on skin.

Mary Sexson

Shadows

The house I grew up in
broods, its broad shadow
the ragged beard
of a prophet.

I am here
to sort through things
left behind by my parents.
They are my things now,

yet when I sit in mom's rocker
or hold dad's coffee mug
or open a dresser drawer,
I feel like an intruder.

Even the silence
that settles everywhere
like a fine mist
is theirs, not mine.

In a shoebox I place
faded black-and-white photos
that divide childhood
into rectangles of time.

I take them with me,
tucking my shadow
under an arm,
closing the back door.

David Lee Garrison

Hokusai I: "The Great Wave off Kanagawa"

It's grinding roar, all contradiction and mystery,
dangerous and seductive, so wild and sure.

Swimming through alarms of flight and struggle,
muscular arms from the depths. The wave sucks

in, then flings out. It ceases, desists, yet never stops
beginning. Sometimes I can only hear its perfidy.

Hokusai's wave wrecks fishermen's boat and lives.
I watch from the shore. I watch from the bow.

Sometimes I'm certain the wave is watching me
as I watch, futilely trying to learn from the master.

His wandering life, ninety houses and fifty names.
He gave up on changing the oceans.

He wrapped his brush around the ferocious
waves of the sea. Its cadence dares, screams.

Don't put yourself in that catastrophic canvas—
Ishmael will not save you.

W. Hans Miller

Hokusai II: "Maple Leaves on a River"

Hungry and teetering, famous
for publicity, scam, coinless again.

Hokusai made a challenge. Buncho, his rival,
accepted the wager, all or none.

No chance with the master's wide sweeps
of soaked azure on giant paper,

an unwilling rooster's bloodred feet dancing
on the cerulean surface.

All the booty found Hokusai's pockets,
braggadocio for his "picture of the floating world."

Without a yen in a week's time,
yet master of the future.

W. Hans Miller

Among the Azaleas

Inside the house of the azaleas
is a room so tiny only a child
could hide, giggling and dreaming
with a peanut-butter-smeared face

while big people in the big room
shout words about paying bills
or passing bills or illicit thrills,
martini juice dripping from their eyes.

And each night the yellow porch light
beckons the small child outside to moon
among the azaleas. All he knows are
crayons, rhymes, and secret promises

never to grow up in their world.

James Nolan

The Bad Luck Child

did not know the charm grafted to the sole of his foot.
In time, he met the mascara-faced man
and the woman with the tattooed smile.
His day brightened with the first snow,
his scar changed color with the thaw,
but he could not understand its purple and green,
its red to yellow,
the fold of skin at his heel,
the fractures of bent toes and injured toenail.
When he took his first lover, everything saddened within him,
and when she left him months later,
he cried night after night.
Only the first snow in the year of the child soldier
pulled him away,
and he went on living,
one century changing to another.
He fell in love with sad-faced clowns,
had many bad luck children,
never ceased at the wonder of first snow.
The river changed course twice in his lifetime,
the bottom of his foot able to find every rock to cross,
every foothold to keep from drowning.
The wisdom of his foot,
the markings of eyeliner and dark rouge,
the long lines he recited and the short ones he wrote down,
the way a smile is a frown:
the prophesy of birthright did not come to pass.

Michael H. Brownstein

In the Attic

Some things are better left in the past,
buried under decades of fallen leaves,
slowly turning into soil and worm feed.
But clearing out my childhood home
to sell it and divide the proceeds
forces memories to surface for one
last gasp of air:

The third-grade report card with
my teacher's handwritten comment "sourpuss"
reminds me that my best friend moved away that year.
The thumb-sized dolls I used to play with in the corner
of the living room by the radiant heater,
warming myself behind the furniture
and learning to be content alone.
My older sister's vinyl record albums
I listened to with her chunky headphones
while she was out—Simon and Garfunkel
consoling me for not being invited
to the movies with the popular crowd.
There are good memories, too:
A silky blue ribbon I won in a local art contest.
The high school variety show program.
(Flowers planted on history's grave?)
Singing in the school choir, sculpting in the art club—
ready-made companionship with people
who shared at least one common interest.

This group solution also applies in adulthood,
where long hours at work fill weekdays.
A hiking club reliably provides trail adventures
for two weekends per month,
and the annual block party and passing hello's
during daily dog walks all administer
social interactions in measured doses—
not too frequent, not too long—
just right for the little girl in the corner of the room,
just enough to keep my mind in the present
as I walk the ridge between socialite and hermit,
now in the attic,
sorting memories alone.

Connie S. Tettenborn

Murmuration of Starlings

I.

My namesake, a chunky bird
making a four-pointed star
thousands soaring together

II.

Pinwheels, pitchforks, incarnations
rivers of pepper floating in skies of blue
Dame Fortune bidding the stakes

III.

Shivering, shaking loose the sky
of thorns, plummeting as one
like scimitars, then gone

IV.

Silly humans. Can't fly, never
could. The bloodiest fools
staring upward in envy.

V.

The vinegar rises, and they are impelled to answer
Nature is the simple reason, sexual calling
another, we don't know—the truth

VI.

N=i0tfw2 might be the answer
The formulae are as meaningless
as your conjectures

VII.

From horizon to horizon, the vertical air
beating against their wings and a sound of fluttering
magnified to a boom as they launch ever higher

VIII.
These bird brains—how do they communicate? who
is the leader? why don't they bang into each other
as they wheel in unison with precision and speed?

IX.
Filled with passion and joy, they never stop
to think about it; the slightest riffle and they drop into fields
calling them home

X.
The starlings are in the lost grain, and even
in the cities of late, creating havoc and chaos
out of the whistle and shriek of beauty

XI.
These are the seven things I wonder about:
the snakes that flame before the total eclipse of the sun;
the chartreuse of the aurora borealis;

XII.
the bottom half of a double rainbow; music and sounds
that are conceived in the mind; river stones
like *suiseki* that carry a memory

XIII.
the bifurcation of light spiraling
out of the darkest of pits,
and the murmuration of birds

Stella Ling

Learning How to Sing

Ears truly open / you hear the Earth's voice.
   A baritone / geologic depth and range.
      Birch leaves unfurl in the key of G
         while samaras of red maples drop
in A minor / waving farewell to
    lower branches / April breezes run
       scales ending at high C / which raise
        the hairs on my forearm.
Ears closed / missed notes and options
    manifold "shoulds" / vacations not taken / condos
       unpurchased / the child that could have been.
        Life's tune wafts away / ten minutes late / dropped
call / tire flat as a road-killed skunk
    turn right instead of left / shrills like A or C sharp.
       Singing lessons mean open ears / breath
        shakes joy oi oi oi oi oi oi loose
from vocal chords / then zing, zing, zing,
   zing, zo, zo, zo, / my notes in blissful
       synchrony with teacher's ivory keys.
        For twenty minutes I live in a waved
universe of perfect vibration / no me, no
   you / just notes clasped close.

                        Gary D. Grossman

La Vida Puede Estar Sola

Life can be lonely

I hear it long before I can see it.
The four-wheeler roars up the rutted road,
pulling a dusty tail.
The deer and elk will run, but
the sheep just raise their heads,
then return to grazing.

The wide grins of the middle-aged couple
speak of a free afternoon
with no responsibilities
to enjoy the sego lilies and heartleaf
arnica. To breathe the fresh mountain air.

Will my children have a free afternoon
now and then to climb the Andes,
see the flor del Inca, and
watch the llamas because of the
money I send home?

My border collie doesn't stir but tracks the
four-wheeler just as she tracks the sheep—
a sea of salt with a few pepper flakes here and there.
Sometimes Luna bristles and stares.
I search and spot the lurking coyote,
but he's quickly gone.

Only one more year on my H-2A work visa and
then I go home to Peru, wondering
if Alejandro and Jacinta will know me.

Raul comes tomorrow with beans and rice
and will move my trailer farther up
the mountain. My horse can't pull it,
even though it's only twelve feet long.

Tonight while the four-wheeling couple
showers and watches television, will they think
about me? Do they know I paid money to
come to this country? That I am one of the lucky ones?

As I eat, listen to the radio, and study my
Spanish/English dictionary, I will think about
them and wonder if they realize they
are lucky, too. They never have to worry
that their children might not know them.

Lorraine Jeffery

The Invisible Underground Railroad

Most of the travelers who use this railroad have grown sorrowful.
Weary adjunct tears taught them nothing but fear about goals.
They seemed sane when I met them; I said stop the run-away.
Fly away! That is what slaves did who wanted to protect their dream—
they hopped that invisible train. No one knew which way it was going,
only that it was going North. Not a single traveler who had a fear
of ghosts or indeterminacy was ever allowed to board or see travel plans.
Slaves never keep a secret, certainly not the ones who love their master.
They always tell what happens in the quarters, so
I never tell anyone anything I don't want God to know about. I keep what
I know under the belt of my tongue and never let a word
pass the gatepost of my lips.

Herbert Woodward Martin

Ta Nisia

In a window seat above the Aegean,
I dream I return to an island held
in a palm of blue,
my boat in a harbor cradling
the sea.

The plane touches down
in graffiti-smeared Athens,
air soured by diesel,
whines of Vespas,
seasoned by Greek from sidewalk
tables and market stalls
near unearthed stele on city streets,
a language linked with epic
poems, letters on an Attic vase,
rare tongue with an ancient alphabet
fitting for a singular place,
its few speakers a small group
I want to join,
using Greek it's taken years to learn.

I shout over sirens to summon a cab,
share the driver's dislike of traffic and smog,
his love of cool evenings,
his longed-for returns
to his village on Crete.
Symfono, I agree. *Emai mazi sas*—
I am with you, I say,
wanting in,
a floater
seeking a berth, signing his receipt
with the letters of an outlier
tongue.

I miss the ferry to the islands,
grow drowsy as the stern shrinks
in a brownish haze,
check into a Piraeus hotel.
On the rayon bedspread,
I slide into sleep, a collapsed
slab of coastline
adrift
on a mud grey sea.

Lily Jarman-Reisch

The Dwelling

for Mark Strand

The poet inherits a painting
he's not gazed upon in twenty-five years
and realizes now the scene is where,
without regret, he has gone to live:

From outside the cabin,
the interior is ablaze,
for it is late afternoon
and sunlight strikes the west window,

so that, in truth, it is as uninhabited
as a room in an Edward Hopper.
There is snow on the ground around,
and thus to the north, behind.

A gray wind has arrived. Trees
are of all kinds and no kind.
They are trees, naked. Naked also
is the foreground, the near horizon,

transparent as the glass that traps it
yet, from the other side, perhaps
black as the back of a mirror,
a lane stretching there from the cabin

to no particular place, half abyss,
or, in another season,
a morass. And there,
there are his eyes on him.

Karl Elder

Madam Houdini

Going grey and blurring
into background like the colourless
clouds of sea and sky smudging
the horizon as you squint into
yet another weary day.
     Jawline, eyelids slightly
drooping, and taut, smooth stretch
of skin you never imagined
would dry or wither, loosening
and beginning to line.
     It's taken time,
but now abundantly clear
through shop assistant's opaque
eyes, strangers on the street,
that you are fading into furniture.
That chair, that shelf, that table
still functional but outdated,
ready for replacement.
Sometimes invisibility
serves purpose. You can weave
and walk among without detection,
     without harassment,
without the pressure to shine.
But it's still strange to be unseen,
     moving like mist
into your final disappearance.

Kate Maxwell

Borderline in 1982

I knew I was in trouble.
Flowing along the long tarmac line
where cowboys sling granddad-colts and
move in packs like watchful wolves
with thin thumbs out in a hazy row,
faces gaunt, young eyes squinting.
Denim shirts too tight, hats too hot,
stained, salty with grime and road sweat,
and feet gummed in scuffed-boot slime.

And I, in a shirt of checked cotton,
backpack new, a too-obvious orange,
startled into some vague terror
as the sun seared my neck Texas red.
An old jackal stopped, limped away.
I looked hard, but it dissolved into air.
Trucks with fender horns blared by,
sixteen-wheelers thundering a song
as I tried hard to look like I belonged.

Then came night, a purple haunt,
and truck stop neon pulled me in.
I sipped at a strong coffee, gritty and cold.
It cost me a dollar, a greasy donut, too,
then I went to the very edge of the night.
Later, I stood under a faint, flickering sign.
A blue-light trooper stopped, then stared,
and I turned into some southern saint with
arms out—a cross in the hot moonshine.

I walked into the night's dark edge
feeling low, part of the distance
as a new semi, lit with luck, stopped.
Two women steeped in love and hope—

one fierce, one an angel with orbs for eyes—
offered me a ride for a little gas money.
They were running from brutality and the past,
heading for California, land of everything.
We sped along, each counting some cost.

They dropped me off, and I rolled into El Paso
and on to Juarez, town of bright shadows.
The sheriff, swung low with pistols of silver,
called me *sly gringo*.
The mescal bars, lined with drains of grey,
had a cold, deadly allure; color came later.
Beauty wore moist make-up, not much else.
The night was filled with sighs and stranger sounds.

I staggered out into the morning, sick and spent,
and caught the border bus heading further west.
Met some loving people along the highway,
but others scared me. Some warned me not to stare.

Carmel, Los Angeles, Santa Cruz, San Francisco—
names to call the stars and undiscovered planets.
The Pacific held me tight. I felt full, immersed;
ate something that made my mind shimmer.
In the end, I said goodbye, moving back east,
although something said *stay, there's more*.

Ryan Cresswell

For Orion Isaac Feig

As I read of Nero in a cavernous bar
among lazy drunks with murderous gray eyes
who wait for gorged wallets to fall, or any coin
fumbled away to find them ever wanting more.
I thought of Orion, a poet of that sliding edge
which mental illness jostles with savage glee,
leaving him homeless, sleeping like an aroused owl,
washing off dirt in bar toilets or gas stations.
Where a stranger might be kind with dollars.
The gaping holes in his pants would not keep long.
A street poet, some hacks misnamed him then.
To me, an emperor of regal vitriolic verse
who slept nights in parks and alleyways with
one eye half open that saw the world.

Rp Verlaine

My Life in Cannabis, Complete

1.

Tenth grade and my virgin entrance
into the circle of pals sharing a hash pipe,
way-deep in someone's back yard.
The slender thing passed to my hand. First
suck. "Hold it in, man." Toasted throat.
Second time, woody taste in my mouth.
Third time: no one will ever know
why I didn't inhale but puffed into the stem.
Out sailed the pellet, weed lost in the weeds.
Trudged back to the party. Them: disgusted,
underbuzzed. Me: traitor to my generation.

2.

Eleventh grade. Neither the chipped-lip,
ivory-tinted pipe I found by the roadside,
nor the baggie of odd plant matter I'd saved
just to discover how it might smoke,
survived Mother's shaken voice,
Dad's pickaxe stare. And I'd hidden them
so carefully under an undershirt.
Lost the chance to make myself sick
from whatever-it-was tamped in the bowl.

3.

At thirty, on the Sargasso Sea of busted
love lives. My latest non-strategy
to entice her beyond unbudged friendship:
abandon the unstoned life. Join her in Js
on city saunters, after plays, after dinner.
Some will claim I didn't smoke often enough,
didn't hold the burn deep enough.
Yes I did, and yes I did. Alas, zero.

My mind stayed as unblown as ever,
my Third Eye complacently shut,

until the double-header: marijuana
before a late-afternoon movie,
second joint afterward. I homed
to my swinging-bachelor pad, sledge-
hammered. Fell face first on the sofa bed.
Woke in pitch dark in all my clothes,
a real man of my generation at last.

David P. Miller

Solastalgia

a family gathers smiling
in this photo not yet sepia
someone not yet missing
a routine document
of ebb and flow

we had wax wings
a common metaphor
of earnest self-importance
grand and vague
yet melting near a cold star

in a solitary confinement of self
and far off country of dream
I think I keep seeing you
I see you everywhere

what is past remains past
my heart is on the outside
how can I be homesick
while being home

Les Bernstein

Days Dedicated to Something

—Oliver Whang, "The Dog (et al.) Days,"
National Geographic, August 2021

Dear Mr. Whang,

I get it: some holidays are designed to save
vultures and rats from infamy; others to applaud
olives, escargot, jellyfish, pigmy hippos,
the Heimlich Maneuver, and hazelnut cake.

You inspired me to track Fat Bear Week,
and what's the happenchance Sea-Monkey Day
falls on May 16? I'll raise my birthday glass
to those briny shrimps and toast their resilient

usefulness. What if I lobbied Congress
for Poets Rejected 100 Times a Year,
Women of a Certain Age Who Still Dye Their Hair,
and Lovers of Hulu and Netflix?

Would the UN care to raise consciousness
about Live Sand Dollars on Oregon's Shores
or the Extinction of Rational Humanoids?
Let me know if this sounds feasible.

By the way, my calendar notes today
celebrates "Women's Equality."
I suspect you'd agree one day a year
is never enough for anything.

Carolyn A. Martin

Sight Shifting

A reprobate   from Dante's hell   sneers
from tiles   on my bathroom floor
Roman nose   gaunt cheeks   hair   blending
into caulk   unnerved   he wants   to know
what right   I have   to stare   at   his suffering

*

Standing on   our Persian rug   I watch
deft hands   interlacing   warps and wefts
tying knots   one by one   row by row
what's more   magical   multi-color   geometry
or tribal tales   looming   in the weave

*

How would Monet   see   my summer yard
if I take   my glasses off   pink petunias blur
with fuzzy   blue stock   white aster-clusters
intertwine   while dozen shapes   of shade
play   beneath   a smudged maple tree

*

Linus saw Mozart   in the sky
Charlie Brown   a rubber duck
Copernicus   a sun-centered   galaxy
untouted   Aristarchus   planets
swirling   methodically   in 230 BCE

*

I've told   my story   so many times
the plot flows   with fine-tuned   imagery
bits   of mystery   energize
multi-worlds hidden behind my eyes
shifting hints   longing   to be seen

Carolyn A. Martin

Sandcastles Without Children

It hadn't always been like this.
I used to be a skinny runt, sobbing
and refusing to come down for dinner,
my mouth bandaged to stop me singing.

I used to be delighted
by the surprise of each new dawn.
But it became difficult to meet people,
empty day after empty day.

Now the moon shines alone in the sky.
I can see it through hotel windows.
I'm a sleepless stranger in a port
where my ship might soon be sailing,
honky-tonking in the harbour,
another self just around the corner,
loosed from my bonds
with the bandaged and the lame
who set about each other.

I wonder how alone we all were,
building sandcastles without children
while the sea shone.

Richard Moore

Walking Above Treetops

This happens mainly in my dreams,
with no catheters, no shrinks to replace
what was paralyzed by war.
The leaves there are of helium hues,
the shades of Arles August.
Branch tips reach on & on,
not as arms but river reeds.
The clouds are Monet's pads,
palm-wide with welcome.
Before the draft, I studied art,
& sometimes now in this chair,
Life's dream returns legs & loins
in the lines of brushstrokes,
in pigment parachutes.

Here's the elevation of love made
on parchment-abandon,
& here, too, is a Rockettes show
above where landscapes are still
for my passing effortless.

Pinch this thigh; I won't be stirred.
Slap this other &, yonder yet,
I'll be breathing wild blue.

Stephen Mead

A Table in Rome

Seated at a table meant for two,
without a phone, my eyes have no mission.
They avoid intrusion, but long for contact.

Conversations pound the air,
firing rockets right through me,
shattering my solo strength,

but I'm invisible, so no one knows.

When everyone is seated, three stars
appear in the skies over Rome and
words become Friday night prayers.

Unable to pray where I am,
I imagine searching for you
after a bombing in wartime,
walking over mounds of dusty bricks
thinking you must be there.

I glance at the door,
but, of course, you don't walk in.

Sitting at the table meant for two,
I collect my broken pieces and look up
to a server's smile.

His soft words wash over me
as he hands me the menu
with its promise of a Sabbath meal.

Mimi Rosenbush

The Penny Pinchers

I remember the constant penny-pinching,
as a first-generation Canadian,
that family obsession with saving,
and how splurging was a bad word.

I remember how *mamá* couldn't get work for years,
because her university degree wasn't recognized,
until that job she finally landed at a daycare,
then lost when my brother got chicken pox.

I remember wanting Levis and brands other kids wore,
while wearing the dresses *abuelita* stitched for me,
or ducking into second-hand shops,
long before thrift stores were cool.

I remember taking city buses to school,
sneaking in the back to avoid paying the fare,
trying to slip through on last month's pass,
and biking before climate change was a thing.

I remember weekly dinners 'out' at McDonalds,
later upscaled to sit-down restaurants with folding menus,
and family vacations camping or road trips at cheap motels,
besides our sacred trips back to Chile every few years.

I remember making dollhouses from old boxes,
eating food past the marked expiry date,
cutting sunscreen in half to salvage remnants,
and reusing creased Christmas wrapping paper.

Some are things I still do today,
many years and bank accounts later,
despite all logic, because I feel guilty about waste,
and scarcity leaves scars long after needs are met.

Jen Ross

An Exact Copy of Jesus

Jesus came to our door.
She was dressed like a boxer in warmups,
all in black.
She said she had to pee real bad,
could she please use our bathroom.

Jesus was wearing a stocking cap pulled down
low over her ears.
Her face was round and brown as a blood moon
through wildfire smoke,
eyes like a wounded cow.

Jesus said her name was Jones.
She came to our door in the second year
of the pandemic, in the blast of winter.
Anyone could be a vector, carry the weapon
that would put us on a ventilator,
cause us to suffocate
alone with just the beeping machines.

Jesus smelled like a dead animal, clothes stained
and crusted, hands covered in gloves of dirt.
She said she had an interview.
She said she had a dossier.
She said she'd been the victim
of identity theft.

Jesus said *What a nice house*
as she passed through the front room,
eyeing the empty couch.
Are you Buddhist? she asked.

Jesus slept out front on the cold concrete,
fully clothed inside my sleeping bag,

beneath the star quilt hand-stitched by my grandma.
In the morning, prayer flags fluttering overhead,
she sat there on a folding chair,
wrapped in old fabric,
arguing with the air.

After two days, Jesus walked away with nothing
but a rucksack. We disinfected everything,
smudged the house, washed the quilt and bag
three times in soap and vinegar. At breakfast,
we talked about how we might have let
the virus in, how even though we're vaxxed
we both could die
of kindness.

Jesus left a wrinkled note under a rock
on the patio, scratched in shaky script, blurred
with what must be tears.
Thank you for your trust, it read.
Thank you for seeing me as I am.
I'll come again
after I get the job.

Wayne Lee

Loneliness

It eats at the heart—
rodent, parasitic,
gnawing, sucking at the innermost.

The big dramas, the shock of loss,
of deaths and departures ...
even as you weep, you know tears will cease.

But loneliness goes on and on. It nourishes itself,
flourishes on silence, emptiness,
fungi colonizing an abandoned house.

Such a wonder it is to watch my species laugh together
in the café where I sit by myself,
stuck where I can't find my way out.

The leaning across a table, the teasing, jokes, the gossip,
arguments, mock arguments, the gathering close
for hurts needing to be told, for joys it is a joy to speak.

In this solitary place,
walls hear nobody but me.
The words, sounds, songs I utter
return to the silence they arose from
and deepen it. There is a sense of being sucked into
an unfathomable hole.

Put on a symphony, talk to God,
make a list, be busy. Yes—here I am, being busy.
Anything to fill the enormously long days
in which I am the only human being there is to talk to;
days in which loneliness
keeps eating at my heart.

Emmanuel Williams

Mango Selling in Manhattan is Dangerous

Six mangoes swayed, supported by the green
hammock of her worn homespun skirt. Free fruit
offered for stolen kisses. She was twelve,
the vendor old and married. Mom won't ask,
assuming she shinnied boldly down the trunk,
negotiating risks all girls must take,
the rash continuum of poverty
attached unseen to her identity.

Alicia can't explain her happy face,
her realization that beauty's prized,
how secrets feed a hungry family.

Remembering his pile of mangos, cupped
like sacraments, its paper-leather rind,
no snake of conscience hibernated then.

She watched her brothers lick their fingers, lips,
lost in a delirium of orange flesh,
aware contentment crooned a lullaby,
aware adults preferred what's left unsaid.

Soon she'll embrace the kin of Sisyphus,
who heft the weight they bear eternally
instead of facing darkness just ahead.

Today's transactions on a Queens' train tapped
that memory, unpeeling older fruit,
sweet, satisfying inner core explored.

Then roughly she is grabbed, her mango cart
possessed by men in blue who handcuff her.

Much worse, Alicia's strip-searched, ticketed,
detained; her merchandise confiscated.
She's unlicensed to sell on the subway.

New York's Mayor will say they're stopping crime.

Hate crimes continue to rise (and assaults)
while officers are tackling temptation—
aware forbidden fruit in callous hands,
cut, scored, cored, and juiced can lead to perdition.

Preventing public sinning requires more
than shame—pursuing like a trail of ants.

LindaAnn LoSchiavo

Illustration by LindaAnn LoSchiavo

Enigma

Inspired by a viewing of Emily Brontë's account book as part of the private collection at The Brontë Parsonage Museum. It is seldom displayed but intrigues academics and researchers alike with its cut-out pages.

Page edges are marbled,
    onyx oblong, banal,
        you search for my traces in torn-off stubs,
            cut short, obtuse, self-effaced, debased,
                racing towards the otherworld,
                    a slippage in time allows your hands to hold mine,
                        where mine have been between two hundred years,
                            slender but strong enough to pummel Keeper
and winch myself around deadening furniture as my lungs gave out.
Can you glean my nature from your salt-spiked fingers which linger
grasping through ink-dim mahogany shelves?
My lips curl at your folly, trying to breathe
a clockwork bellows animation into my objects so I may rise,
necromancer, Minerva, Lazarus, on the cusp of existence, summoned
thus to answer your very many many many questions.

Emma Conally-Barklem

Gone Stale

I tasted an expired sunset.
It used to be mine,
a fired sky, framed
in hill and dale,
an event knowable in moments
that shape the dark
with memories of
a world bathed in sun,
golds that bleed
to purpled night.

But this dirt has forgotten
the shape of my passing shadow,
and I failed to bite
into the beauty
when I was fresh
enough to taste it best.
Its familiar surrender
has become burlesque,
an old routine I wish
I still loved so much
as when it was new.

Chris Hasara

Bookaholic

So what if I hang around bookstores—
in my neighborhood, around the city, and
look them up on vacations in new places?
I get a buzz from books.
There's something about a hardcover
that's like downing a few shots of Jack Daniels.

At home I bury myself in my fix—
It's always the same, I get comfortable
and end up with one book in front of me
after another until daylight's closing time.
Past partners begged me to find help.
Perhaps my habit is out of control—

in underwear drawers, in my briefcase,
on the couch, under the seats in my car,
piles in my kitchen and inside cabinets,
slipped between bedsprings and mattress.
When I cracked open another, lovers cringed.
They knew they'd find me passed out
with another one in my lap.

Lylanne Musselman

Part of the Picture
(inspired by a line from *Crossing Brooklyn Ferry* by Walt Whitman *)*

I, too, felt the curious abrupt questioning stirring inside me,
watching the crowds processing beneath my balcony
in carnival parades of costumes and painted expressions,
their excitement and fears and fevered aspirations
all coalescing in a murmuring meltwater confluence
of torchlight shiftings, flurries of sounds and faces
spilling and pouring from the backstreets and side streets,
from car parks and alleyways and the lantern glow of pubs,
from the reek and tang of brewing and fermentation,
from the coiled springs of suppressed violence,
those fierce, fickle blooms of fellowship and tribal loyalties.

I, too, shared their shifting collage of expressions,
their mood swings of rage and euphoria and despair,
watched torchlight play on foreheads and cheekbones,
saw dark pockets of shadow behind their eyes,
some of them motioning for me to join them
as I wavered, standing above the streetlamps
halfway up in the clouds, fearful of letting life pass me by.

Still not quite finding myself part of the picture,
still locked within this bonehouse body of mine,
this livewired matrix, this neural-sparked circuiting of arteries and
veins,
red cell/white cell/blood/corpuscles race within me.
It's all me me me—this inner eye of growing awareness,
this ego id of chemical-sparked alchemy
that sets me adrift from the rest of creation,
trapped like an insect in amber, cut off from everything,
stirring beneath me, letting the procession pass me by.

Once I thought I almost belonged
to these shifting landscapes of streets and houses:

the distant rattle and chunter of traffic along the seafront,
the dwindling murmurs of tears and laughter,
the sounds of all those faraway voices processing inland
in spiral skelters and drifts of leaves and salt-tanged gusts of breeze.

I leave it all to find the sky
flowing in great churning rifts and furrows of cloud,
stretched and rib caged as if racked in pain,
all scurrying eastward,
sweeping away these muffled debris of sounds,
these fading echoes of music and laughter,
these dwindling confusions of rage and layers of desire.

Cosmo Goldsmith

Dis-Ordered or Simply Eccentric:
Who Gets to Name Us?

Must touch/count-out each fingertip
thumb to pointer thumb to index thumb
to twice married finger thumb to wee pinkie
One   two   three   four
reverse and repeat
complete the sequence
in full
before the bus reaches street-light? Before
the girl in the blue wool coat looks my way?
It's so arbitrary
Anxious? You bet!
Here comes that spoon again
It's a sorcerer's apprentice spoon
imaginary
never-ending
ever-filling-spoon Must fill it drink it/fill it drink it/
fill it drink it/fill it drink it (Type of liquid not important)
Must take liquid into mouth from spoon Must
drink all liquid to keep spoon dry before the next red
post box? The next small dog with human?
It's so arbitrary
Oh I could go on!
I must
rattle an' rattle the metal letter box tink-t-tink-
t-tink-tink Must announce arrival then
go straight to bedroom Flick on/off/on/off/on/off/
flick/flick/flick light-switch Do not be fooled
finger pressure not simply sequence is key!
Must not say *bye-bye-puss* to cat—Ever!
Cannot risk the thing
The thing?
(It's so arbitrary)
Please be quiet
I am so tired
Why must
my foibles
be labelled?

Lorraine Gibson

Ipsissimus

Fiddling with twiddles on some fancy temple,
moaning orgasmically, "This is amazing,"
while bemused natives gather, uncertain
whether to look at the camera or you,
doesn't impress, *Adrasteia*. Your books,
TV series, accolades, weighed in the balance
are wanting because you don't mention the most
remarkable, gemlike, iconic construction:
the big cooling tower in the center of Stockport
(sadly demolished back in the seventies)
Dave and I christened The Mayor's Pepper Pot.

Well done, *Dysponteus,* you rowed single-handed
across the Atlantic—a tour de force. *But*
I've one simple question, fairly rhetorical:
have you, my friend, having launched off the slipway
at Lower Town quayside into the calm
but quite swelly briny shielded by breakwaters,
told by the cox, "Come forward to row,"
been bumped in the back by Suzanne in the bow?

Poor *Meliboëa*, despite your success,
prizes, prizes, collections, collections,
accolades, motorcades, five-star reviews,
you're laboring under the terrible burden
of not having written that witty and elegant
haiku that showed how the author's camellia
didn't collapse even though he was stressed.

Don't get me started on you, *Dexamenus.*
Oscars for acting *and* scriptwriting, yes,
rogering movie stars, shooting the rapids,
flying a biplane, breeding chihuahuas,
owning a castle, owning an island,

owning Picassos and Brancusi bronzes—
all that I'm asking is: have you a cat
called Louie? *The Life of the Fly* by H. Fabre?
Had the good fortune to sleep with my wife?

Let's praise the achievements of all the above
who mastered the blockage, impediment, obstacle,
grave disadvantage of *not being me.*

Alex Barr

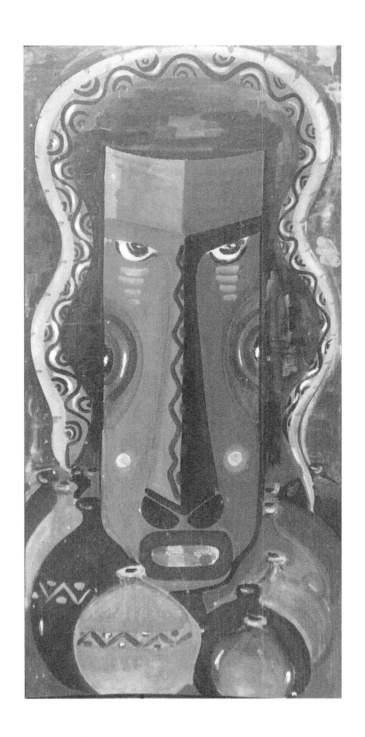

Dufusyokelsplat

Don't believe everything you read.
—Socrates

In an effort to ingratiate yourself, you gush over
the checkout lady's name. *Mariam, so melodic,*
so original! In the midst of your obsequious display,
you drop the dozen eggs she's handed you and watch

the albumen, yokes, and shattered shells ooze over
your shoes and coat the tile so that every step you take
spreads the slippery splatter over the supermarket floor
and out into the parking lot. You watch Mariam's

expression morph from grudging tolerance to hateful
despair, a transformation that makes her question not only
why she needs this job but why she was ever born. You
have committed a Dufusyokelsplat, so named after Colonel

Rufus William Dufusyokelsplat, a lost-to-history Confederate
commander during the American Civil War, who led a charge
against Yankee troops at Chickamauga in 1863 that would have
succeeded had his horse, Butch, not developed a severe case of

back-door trots, thereby handing this important victory to his
boss, General Braxton Bragg. Disgraced by Butch who, the night
before the battle, nosed into the cook tent and ate inordinate
amounts of baked beans, butter, and lard, Dufusyokelsplat finished

his days as an assistant embalmer for a Tennessee undertaker. You
ponder how Dufusyokelsplat became not even a footnote to history,
and you think about yourself who, a few years after your death,
no one will remember—as if you'd never been here, as if you'd

never held the one you love in close embrace, danced with her
against the throng, taught a young boy to swing a bat or pitch
a tent, or, while desperate to impress someone you didn't know,
dropped a dozen eggs in a grocery store and made a mess.

Charlie Brice

Ice Jam

And now, at seventy-two, I wonder when my brain
　　　　began its revolt in earnest.
Was it at a writer's retreat in the nineties
　　　　when I saw my wife standing
with her back turned to me, talking
　　　　to some fellow writers, and I
slipped behind her and squeezed her
　　　　left butt cheek only to discover
how outraged a different woman with
　　　　the same build could become? Or
was it just recently when I couldn't remember
　　　　the name of the "prophet" everyone
swore by in the late sixties? No, it wasn't
　　　　the guy who invented Scientology (what's
his name?), it wasn't Nostradamus—the fellow
　　　　I couldn't remember died in the nineteen forties.
It certainly wasn't Ken Kesey, the name that invaded
　　　　my consciousness and prohibited me
from conjuring any other name. (Why couldn't
　　　　it be Ken Kesey? Maybe all that
electric Kool-Aid altered his neurons, enabled
　　　　him to see into the future like the dude
whose name I couldn't remember.) I was so
　　　　frustrated that I stomped my feet, but
couldn't Rumpelstiltskin the name into my psyche.
　　　　It wasn't until hours later, in the middle
of detailing the recipe I use to make turkey soup—
　　　　the gobbler's carcass, of course, immersed
in my huge white soup pot with garlic, bay leaf,
　　　　onion, carrots, celery, and the magic
ingredient hot curry powder—that the name
　　　　came to me—Edgar Cayce. Maybe
the word "magic" did it. I don't know. My
　　　　wife and I call this process of remembering
breaking-up the ice jam—the name pops up
　　　　out of nowhere and you get to return to
the illusion that you're not so old, that your
　　　　mind is just fine, that everything will be okay.

Charlie Brice

Like You

"People like you," our teacher began, "never have friends."
The older boy I'd crushed on stood there, and his pal.
Smiles had turned to blows; blows had not stopped.
"People like you never know love."

"People like you think you're smart, but you're not.
You'll never amount to anything. No one will have you.
Every job will fire you." Her face reddened with every word:
"You will be beaten and deserve it." I was eleven years old.

"People like you live desperate, lonely lives and then
find an early, unmarked grave. Save time," she purred,
"and find it now." My next ten years began while the world
mocked. The blows continued. "People like you!" she spat.

Behind her lies, I heard the truth: "Like you."
Not the only one, but one of many.
Not alone. Not alone! *You are not alone.*

David Milley

Dark Morning

I wanted to learn more about the bishop pine,
conifer native to Point Reyes. "Hike among the lanky,
twisted trunks of the bishop pine on an early morning hike,"
Peaceful, I thought, and signed up.

Merrill, our guide, arrived late, wore sunglasses
on the leaden, damp day.
I have a roster here somewhere, she said, shuffling
through frayed backpack stuffed
with unkempt papers, Oakland A's baseball cap,
large packet of Twizzlers.

We're okay, her aide, Lisa, said gently. *We can start.*
Like a sheepdog, Lisa herded the ten of us
onto the trail. She noted California wax myrtle in forest understory.

Blue-green canopy of pine branches overhead
protected us from morning fog drips.

I inhaled moist air deep in my lungs,
glad I didn't shut off my alarm
and sleep through this hike.

The morning was too cool yet
to release the wax myrtle's spicy
scent, but I anticipated its glory.

Merrill became one of the group, joined a few of us
in the rear. She walked gingerly,
a slight limp. Her faded red sweatshirt
covered a lot, but not the bluish-black bruise
on her throat in the shape of long fingers.

My hiking companion reached for Merrill's backpack.
Let me carry this for you.
Merrill's lips moved in a silent *thank you.*
Tears shimmered on her cheeks.

Christy Wise

Birthday Party Parent

She let us protect him
for two hours on a Sunday when he was eight.
Never had she let him out of her sight,
asking that we stay only at the house during the birthday party.
Her son played well the role of a child
walking outside her gaze for the first time in his life.
When we broke her rule
and went down the block to launch rockets,
we unintentionally cut the umbilical cord
now taped onto his belly button
and hanging lazily
like a scab ready to move on.

When we returned, she stood scowling
outside the gate to the house.
Her hand ran across her throat,
eyes boring into mine as I sat behind the wheel,
signaling the dire moment
when her birthing went wrong
and she let him out into the world,
stillborn at eight years old.
These foreigners, she knew,
understood nothing of a mother's bond,
nothing of Chile and all the decades before
that had led her to keep him tethered.

She left the party early,
gripping her son's wrist too tightly.
We laughed nervously, but she was right.
We could not understand
the stench of a toy rocket
smoking in the grass
surrounded by cactus.

Thomas Ferrebee

The Family of Man (1955)

A collection of 503 black-and-white photographs taken by 273 men and women,
amateurs and professionals, renowned and unknown, curated by Edward Steichen
for the Museum of Modern Art in New York

Long past midnight, I'm folded in flannel
and cobwebs as fuzzy as my slippers.
Time stretches   I reorganize 32 archival binders:
10,000 slide negatives, some of my first published photographs.

I set my loupe aside   turning to miserly bookshelves in a
former linen closet. Wedged beside *Audubon Field Guides,*

The Family of Man and its failing spine   mended with ripe lemons.
I shed scales   wade through brittle pages   faces familiar   from afar

sheepherders   farmers   bridge builders   musicians   belly dancers
carpenters   poets   philosophers   canoe carvers   weavers
window washers   landlords   landless   the loved and the wholly lost.

There's so much life in stillness.
Faces help me understand without words.
I see what cameras in 68 countries saw. "I belong here."

I abandon my office chair   join my tribe on the floor.   We braid
cut-pile carpet   clasp gnarled hands   bathe in a new mother's milk

bearing the human condition   membranes of sin, torture, and tears.
Names shouted   spoken for the last time   a thousand angry tongues
in my pocket.

Frogs and crickets soothe dawn's edges   all that's charred and
scraped over turns to barley and wild wheat berries   and we
feel the earth beneath our bare toes.

We flow, flow, flow   restless, spirited, unyielding.

Sherry Shahan

Manifesto of Scattered Notes, Circa 1980s

I.

They put me in a folding chair at a card table next to Allen Drury. The card tables are spread out in the living room because dinner guests outnumber chairs at the dining room table. They put me next to Allen Drury because he won the Pulitzer Prize in Fiction for 616-page *Advise and Consent* in 1960.

Allen Drury doesn't want to talk about being a Senate correspondent for *The New York Times* or keeping an eye on Franklin D. Roosevelt and Harry S. Truman or his "definitive Washington tale." I don't want to talk about writing short stories for sleazy men's magazines. *Adam, Cavalier, Nugget.*

Dinner guests line up in the kitchen to take their suppers from the dishwasher. I should write something brilliant about them taking steaming salmon from the top rack of a dishwasher. I should read *Advise and Consent* or at least think about reading a book about writing or subscribe to *Writers Digest.* I should change the ribbon on my typewriter.

II.

The recipe for steaming salmon in the dishwasher comes from Hulsey Lokey, Chairman of the Board of Host International, Inc. The longtime chair knew a thing or two about preparing aluminum foil meals: meals and beverages delivered to airports and toll roads.

Hulsey Lokey shared a thing or two about crimping salmon in foil and cooking it on the top rack of a dishwasher. Set the dial on the wash cycle, sans soap.

Colleen Moore lifts her crimped aluminum foil pouch from the dishwasher. The silent screen star wears her hair in a fashionable Dutchboy bob, just like in her silent movie *Flaming Youth.* In the 1923 movie, Colleen Moore plays a bob-haired flapper who engages in a ménage-á-trois with her mother's lover. I should watch *Flaming Youth* or at least think about writing a cookbook, maybe something like *Romancing the Soup Bone* or *the Joy of Hot Dogs.*

III.

Colleen Moore seats me at one of a dozen card tables on her patio, next to James Lee Barrett because he wrote *The Greatest Story Ever Told, Smokey and the Bandit, The Green Berets,* and *Shenandoah.* Colleen Moore's cook dishes up crisp-fried slices of Spam and fruit cocktail with jet-puffed mini marshmallows.

James Lee Barrett doesn't want to talk about Hollywood or his 1975 Tony Award for Best Book of a Musical for *Shenandoah.* I don't want to talk about the sleazy story I'm writing about a golf pro (my ex) and his exploits on a fairway with a country club waitress titled "Long Balls and Driving Shafts."

James Lee Barrett laughs when I tell him about the sleazy liquor store on 24th Street across from St. Rose Catholic School where I flip through sleazy magazines looking for my byline. "Editors don't pay unless I ask, and then only if I remember to send them a SASE."

IV.

A friend takes me to Henry Luce III's apartment for a cocktail because Henry Luce III publishes *Time* and *Fortune* magazines. Henry Luce's wife greets us at the apartment door in a floor-length bathrobe and a cap of pink-sponge hair curlers. His wife cradles a tiny white dog with a tiny bow in her curly hair.

Henry Luce III smiles at me from a large, worn leather chair. Heaps of newspapers and magazines sit on the floor by his worn chair. Henry Luce III doesn't want to talk about how many newspapers and magazines he reads a day, and I don't want to talk about the rejection slips from *Penthouse* and *Hustler* tacked to a corkboard wall in my den.

I stand over a newspaper spread on the floor in a corner of Henry Luce III's bathroom. A red plastic fire hydrant sits in a corner of the spread-out newspaper. Maybe I should read a page of the newspaper while I sit on Henry Luce III's toilet or at least think about writing a story about a thirty-year-old who writes short stories for sleazy men's magazines and never knows what to talk about.

V.

I plop quite independently onto rust-orange shag carpet across a coffee table from Dale McRaven because he wrote episodes of *The Odd Couple, The Dick Van Dyke Show,* and *Laverne & Shirley.* Dale McRaven doesn't want to talk about his Emmy nominations for *Mork and Mindy* or creating the award-winning TV series *Perfect Strangers,* and minutes tick into hours, and it's getting harder and harder for me to know what to say.

I should have joined EST when I had the chance, or at least find something to do with my hands. I write *erasable paper* and *paper clips* on my wrist and am mortified with myself and rub my wrist over my stone-washed jeans.

VI.

It's exhausting being mortified most of the time and scared all of the time and trying to think of something to say. Maybe I should write about being mortified and scared or at least check the *Los Angeles Times* to see if they printed my "Letters to the Editor" about cooking meals in a dishwasher. But never mind.

It's exhausting standing in the sleazy liquor store on 24th Street and thumbing through sleazy magazines, looking for my byline. So I sit at my desk in the godawful silence and half-dark pulling typewriter keys from my mouth, the keys that always ask *Who are you? What do you want? What are you afraid of?*

Sherry Shahan

self-portrait as a local bus

Hijra are intersex people, transgender people, or eunuchs from the Indian subcontinent, residing in communities that follow a special kinship system, creating family for themselves.

after the classes, crushed
like the paper teacup in my
side-pocket, I watch as the bangles
warble through my oesophagus
and into my
belly—a dream, dreams
tattooed down her
back.
Freckled jaw and slender
hips and hyacinth hair, I
claim her. Mine, my,
my sister: a thread
-bare purse held close
to her saree-veiled heart.
They look away, fingering
moustaches and plaits as if they
didn't watch as the other sisters put evening
flowers in her hair at the stairs outside the
subway station like morsels of a prayer. They quick
-ened their pace, but she never goes in there
anyway. Because she climbs into my breast
-bone, chiming. Her hands on the grooves
of my heart. *Spare a few*, she says, *for this* অনাথ. Orphan.

Did you bury them, I wonder, *sister?*
Or did they bury you?
You know I always
keep loose change for you. Get candy or morning
flowers before they rot, cloying
like candy. It was never mine to keep
anyway. I am but a vehicle

for God's loose change. Your hand on my
head, a roof unfurled. Sister, they buried me when
I told them, too.
Someday, teach me how to drape a saree
the way our sister
-mothers shielded you.

Sarah Aziz

Flash

-After Jim Harrison's "Sunlight"

After hours of stormy darkness, I've learned to expect
a flash of saffron sun
docks and departs through a sucker hole
faster than the light and douse of a candle,
that old flare of optimism dashed.
I know the moon can block the sun,
launch us into moments of totality,
but what are the gifts of this wholeness?
At the Sitka ferry terminal, few passengers wait,
pass the time in the shelter of dry vehicles
pecking out texts that will fail to send without connection
to a world that is larger than a tweet.
Outside, ravens take shelter as
the sleet drums a steady rhythm
on an empty ferry positioning itself to a ramp
that will take us from this winter place to another.
We are as cynical as our fathers, a lineage
of men refusing the warmth of light on their faces.

Kersten Christianson

New Girl in the Bookstore

She walked in one day, asking for work,
suspiciously free of tats and slouch,
a girl from another planet.

On break, the staff somehow got on religion.
There were once-Catholics, a lapsed Methodist,
two Jews, and a guy who believed in early Joan Baez.

But the girl said she worshipped Entropy and Coincidence,
and proved it one day when they came to work
to find all the books sorted by color.

When they fanned out and took second looks,
they found spots of genius and joy
amid all the juicy juxtapositions.

Franklin Pierce presided over a blue section
with Cher and Gumby, and a white section
had Lennon and Lenin and the *Wild Plants of Arkansas*.

Soon they were all just browsing and admiring and
laughing and wondering why this wasn't
the from way beginning have the should been it.

Thomas R. Willemain

Intimate Stranger, Marie van Goethem

My lower spine is killing me,
traipsing through the national gallery,
temple of culture. All hushed
reverence baked into the paintings,
not scrutinized, redrawn, scraped,
fretted for, dry brushed, scumbled.

We circle Michelangelo's sculpture
The Slaves twisting out of marble,
scan torsion of flesh and rib,
know only how he captured them
forever writhing. Nothing of cages,
owners, or households, or if they fought in the ring.

I know modern-day slave descendants.
I am one, from millennia past.
Dare I say this aloud? I own this
quantum radiance of their struggle.
Raised to admire stone muscle
turning on bone in museums,
picture streams of sweat, sheaves of breath.

Passing Greek gods, Roman leaders, mute
as we study chisel marks, abrasions—
tools carve illusion into reality. Eyes gouged
for pupils. No clues to their thoughts.
Not robed in purple or red.
Black, gray, white rock.

Or as Degas sculpted young Marie,
fourth position at rest, real linen sagging,
slippers real satin. Some things known.
Poverty and promise. Paris Opera Ballet.
The male gaze, patrons, favors.
One day dismissed. Too often absent.
Then vanished. Silent Marie,
bronze copies worldwide, almost alive.

Lynn Axelrod

Old Friend, Orion

There you are, Orion, old friend.
Although I expected you,
you took me by surprise.
Yes, the air is cooling,
but we've had no frost yet.
Trees have begun to unleaf,
even if the maples are still green.
I happened to be up tonight, nothing unusual,
and saw you in the east, early in your night's watch,
patrolling the wintering skies with your long strides—
your right arm raised in greeting,
your sword asheath—
and welcome you at this time of life
when old friends leave never to return.
I miss my friend of books and discussions of order,
my helpful friend who, tuned in to conspiracy radio,
paced his daily two miles
to quell the conspiracy of a dying heart,
my writer friend who wrote about the Civil War
as if he had smelled the cordite and heard
the screams of wounded horses and men,
and who brought me bags of discarded
library books he bought for fifty cents.
But you are here again, old friend,
and when I patrol my house during late nights
and look out over the roofs and trees,
there you are—
vigilant, reassuring, silent.

John D. Groppe

The Hunter

If I feel physically as if the top of my head were taken off,
I know that is arthritis. She floods every joint.

You have to admire her tenacity.
She laughs through sleepless nights.

Arthritemis the huntress stalks each nerve.
Quaking, I wait for her to go away.

I try to understand. I check my temperature, take my drugs.
At least I know how her visit will go.

My hands, her welcome mat.
My gut, her air mattress.

Somehow, this time, she chomped my ribs.
She made my scalp fall off.

She complains about everything.
We have come to an uneasy accord.

I seek out others like me.
We the hunters, hunted.

On my side, I have kinships.
Friends family doctors mentors strangers—my cat.

I pity her here in my body.
Alone with anxiety, a collagen disorder, a cold.

She does not mind the company she keeps.

Vivian Delchamps

New Moon

In the soft of night, the stars like salt pulled off the table, a sheep turns slowly to me. I kneel to her.

Six seasons pass on the surface of her eye. Luminous wool. Pink shell of ear. All that moves is that which leaves her mouth. Hot breath pushes through cold night.

There is matter waiting inside of me not yet named, and I've come to see it as both still and unfolding. Condensing and dissolving.

I've come again to the dark pasture. There is only moonless wet beneath my feet. Somewhere the sheep breathes and holds her pale face to the dipping sky.

Phoebe Eisenbeis

No Trespassing

My home is a tiny brick house,
solid walls with no windows
except for a one-foot square pane on one side—
my TV without the unnecessary bill—
to watch the world evolve and carry on
as I remain still within my home.
Years flew by, barely noticed,
ivy growing among the stones,
the foundation remaining strong
even among the abusive elements.
Saplings grew into massive trees,
the grass becoming unruly,
hiding my abode from passersby,
perfectly camouflaged
and forgotten.
When you stumble through my threshold,
do not fear when you spy my skeleton
sitting in a rocking chair
gazing out of my small view onto reality.
Speak and then listen
for screams and whispers—
my hopes and dreams
can still be heard
within the stillness
of that tiny brick house.

Kaela Hinton

the journey I remember

earthy odor of nasi goreng, scent
of masala layered with mystery, cinnamon
smoke of incense curling the stone heads of Newari
Gods, fruity musk of humans elbow-to-elbow, jostling
at a full-moon festival, mud of freshly plowed earth
as water buffaloes plop their hooves through rice paddies,
mustard seeds popping in oil, peeled durian stunning your
sense, the soft grassy breath of an elephant trunk beside
my ear, and the dusty smell of a yak sidestepping me
on a rocky trail.

the clamor of crowded streets, horns, beeps, the sonorous
drone of loudspeakers chanting Muslim prayers waking
us at dawn, startling yet soothing, the creak of slick
thin bridge boards as we crossed the Kali Gandaki roaring
like thunder beneath, roughness of sand grains under
toes, wiry scratching bristles of an elephant's hide
against bare legs as I swayed in a howdah, the gentle
snuffle of its trunk seeking peanuts, the cacophony
of unknown birds on a claustrophobic jungle path,
the ching-ching of temple bells at dusk beckoning
worshippers, the swish of wind in fishing nets tossed
over waves, the lingering atonal blend of gamelan
instruments warming up while a monsoon gushed outside
one bamboo pavilion, the floor alive under hands
and feet, the tall grass a living green sky as we hiked
almost-paths, curtaining us like a green waterfall;

the caress of creamy green coconut milk entering my
dry throat, dripping sensual heat of Indian meals
as fingers scooped up vegetables from banana leaf plates,
slurping together as many hands cup rice, alu gobi, daal,
sip chai in jovial union, one unconcerned group chewing,
sweating, burping, no worry over manners to hamper
or deaden pleasure

sweat on my skin, daal entering my
mouth, the pungent flavors of lemon grass or mangosteen
an ether I breathe and move through, senses intoxicated

Jill McGrath

St. Carlos the Melodious

A Found Poem for Carlos Ramirez, 1938-2013*

Went out on his Alvarado Street roof
every morning at seven a.m.
to *crow!*
He was a cloud walking around in pants.
He'd rather be a sparrow than a snail.

He was a teacher who didn't go by the lesson plan,
his presence announcing
that all god's critters sing in the choir.

Listened to his interior self at all costs,
and was never heard to say
an unkind word about another person.

He was like the sun rising from the heart of creation
to bring us joy.
He sang about waltzing bears on his phone machine.

Giving you his full gaze, he'd ask
Who loves you, Baby? then answer
You do!

Poets are many.
Those whose lives are poetry are few.
Carlos was one, forever woven in
to San Francisco's tender tangle.

Remember him by being on the hunt
for all the good things in your life.
Imagine inconceivable joy, then beam
a loving smile to everyone you meet
in his honor.

Kitty Costello

**Gathered, arranged, and embellished from comments made at the memorial
for Carlos at St. Martin de Porres House of Hospitality on Potrero St., 4/21/13.*

Atoms of You

There are still atoms of you
everywhere—
your footsteps on the pavement,
down at your local shopping centre,
under that chair;
on stamps and newspapers;
that skirt, those pants;
the note you wrote to a friend
saying you'd missed her;
the top you gave to your sister.
Atoms of you still linger.

Further abroad,
there are traces of you;
at the Colosseum, perhaps,
a speck or two.
In Bali, a splinter of chicken bone
lies in a corner crack.
You fed the dog who kept coming back.
Patting his mangey head,
"Och, he's just skin and bone," you said.
You're in the book you lent,
the photos that I took,
the texts you sent.

I can't think of you as ash—
ash is what we leave behind when we die,
a hair tint,
a friend's cat, a tree—
but rather as atoms of you,
getting smaller and smaller as the years go by.

Linda Anderson

Other People's Houses

When you live in other people's houses,
it's never clear who exactly rules
your roost. Who will appear
without warning. Who may have keys
to your locks. And, though the rent's
been paid, you feel there's something,
something you're always owing.

You can walk in and find a stranger
in your bedroom fixing a pipe.
You can wake to a near-stranger
at the side of your bed, saying,
"Get up. Your mother's taken ill.
She'll need bedrest for a while; she'll
need looking after. Now be quiet
and get yourself ready for school."
And, trembling, you do, but then
you remember it's Saturday.

In my dreams   *I'm heading down*
a shady road to the large two-story
at the bottom of the hill   it's not
my house   but when I reach it
I walk right in   pass through rooms
empty   or full of surprised faces
I'm not afraid to wander

In my dreams   *the apartment door*
is locked   but they walk right in
people I don't know   drinking
and chatting in the living room
I go into my room and I shut
the doors   over and over

no matter how many times
I can't keep the cat out

Everywhere, the boundaries
keep changing—shorelines
under a moon with tides
you're unable to predict or chart,
the ground under your feet
unsteady and forever shifting.

Melissa Cannon

Queer

queer since birth, when I
changed positions in the womb
and came down the chute
stubbornly crooked

one eye's nearsighted,
the other far,
though how well it can see
into the future's debatable

then there are my Court Cards
   The Fire of Water
   The Water of Fire
try keeping those in the Balance
without falling off the high wire

head in the clouds,
no Earth anywhere in my horoscope,
little wonder I'm broke
and was destined to become a poet

I never could follow the straight
and narrow when there were
so many interesting byways

or follow the prescribed
instructions or do anything
by the book

the first time I picked up
a pair of scissors, I held them
backward in my left hand,
cutting towards myself

as if I always knew I was
a paper doll
to be dressed and redressed
in infinite outfits

with my first chemistry set
my solutions—spontaneous
and homemade—ended up
murky brown sludge

I tuned the strings
of my first guitar to a single
chord and had to sing
every song in its key

that I'm a woman who loves
other women turns out
to be the most normal
thing about me

Melissa Cannon

The Shape of the Sea

It was not the moon that I stared at,
but its reflection,
showing me the faraway shape of the sea

I stood on the promenade alone,
feeling the gentle press
of a sultry Portuguese breeze

I wondered how the cats were,
if they missed us,
if they knew,
were sure,
that we would return to them

My wife and daughter came
to stand on either side of me,
my daughter holding some candyfloss.
"They don't call it candyfloss here, Dad."
"Is that right? What do they call it?"
"I don't know."

I smiled over her head at my wife.
My wife smiled back.
I picked up my daughter and placed her on the promenade wall
and she leaned back against me.
I took a breath

The air was candyfloss sweet,
the moon hung in the sky,
the ocean stretched out before us,
and somewhere beyond it,
the cats were sleeping,
were waiting

Steve Denehan

Inside the Apartment

A bird trap set with a shaky wire where his heart
should be catches purple, red, yellow-plumed
birds that fly out and in again. A terrestrial globe
acquired from a local store, placed on a small table
with a leg about to give way. A six-foot cupboard
piled with lies that never got in the way of a story,
old flight tickets, re-watched cowboy films. An empty
shelf at the bottom where dust spells out, in capital
letters, the names of the people he was careless with.

A painting by his hand of a woman resembling me,
clothed in head-to-toe white, staring into the ocean
with five white birds flying in the distance. It covers
the whole wall. He, leaning over a kitchen counter
coated in layers of cigarette ash. I, fidgeting smilingly
and colouring the silence. *Do you have anything to tell me?*
I leave space for an answer, but he cannot find words.
Except once. *I see parents with their kids now. I wish
I had shown you more affection when you were young.*

Another time: *I hated my father.* I talked about forgiveness.
No words, though he seemed to listen. I retrieved my phone
and scrolled the Birds of Australia Insta page. Every corner
of his face changed. *Pink Robin, Rainbow Lorikeet.* Remember
our aviary, I said. The canaries you turned bright orange.
My eyes seeking one of your stories as purple geraniums
enveloped me. The garden with forgotten coffee spoons
behind the fixed grins of gnomes. A goldfinch with a red
ribbon tied to its leg, trapped and freed by the same hand.

Amanda Anastasi

Opera

The house lights dim
like lanterns fading in a fog. The smell
of paper and rosin under hot lamps in the pit
rises as the music magically whisks
the curtain away.

Jane, is it *Bohème* or *Traviata* tonight?
Or does it even matter?
You've seen each more times than you'll admit,
shifted in your seat, dozed
during those plights and contrivances you know
as well as you know your path
from room to room in your house at midnight.

For years you've wept with Mimi's last breath,
or Violetta's, left the theater haltingly,
still checking your tears.
You buy your ticket with the anticipation
of spending that wet emotion
which you won't display outside.
The need for tears is yours,
you know, not theirs on stage.

You wish yourself the heroine's footlights,
the gallery's adulation, pity, love. I know.
If that's the only part you'll have, with arms
rose-brimmed for you, I wish it too.

James Kangas

Cape Town, 1990

I rode the train to work today,
my first day on the job.
Friends offered to kindly show me
a quick way to get to town.

"Nie man! Kom hier!"
they said, grabbing me by my wrist.
"You can't go there!"
they said, pointing to the sign that read:
"Whites Only/ Slegs Blankes."

They pulled me away
from the pristine first compartment
to the broken-down third class.

I rode the church to work today,
Pastor dancing up and down the aisle,
our congregation packed like sardines
on torn seats, others holding fast
against falling out open doors
while we clickety-clacked along.

People smiled and applauded
as Pastor's words whistled through missing teeth.
He made us forget
the degradation of our skin.

Adiela Akoo

The Comfort of Darkness

Often left home alone after dark,
I was a late-night latchkey kid.
Noises in the house would frighten me,
so I'd turn on every light
in an attempt to dispel
something darker than darkness.
Illumination never worked to bring a feeling of safety,
and with each odd, unknown sound,
my anxiety would grow.
Something was after me.

What does a child do when they are terrified?
No one to call, no place to hide.
Stepping outside into the embrace of shadowed arms
was a contradiction, but
immediately I would feel protected and safe
looking in at the light
until Dad would get home.

Light is often a lie.
Lucifer was the Morningstar,
and God says that He dwells in darkness.
Maybe, just maybe,
those comforting, shadowed arms
were the arms of God.

John R. Hinton

Grieve But Cannot Grieve

after Rodney Jones, *How Much I Loved This Life*

You rise in the light, blistered by light.
Jamaica 1974, we live in the yeast
of Black is Beautiful.

Every moment we scrape awake.
If I lay my hand on your arm, you
jump as if a duppie swept over you.

We cringe in our bed
from the reggae band thumping
all night across our back fence

splintering ears that refuse to listen.
You rise in the light, blistered by light.
Is it the cleft of continents,

undertow of the slave trade
that sears you?
I rise in the light

blistered by your light
that pokes like a detective
into my shadows.

Nancy L. Meyer

Dreaming Jamaica 1974-77

University artist residency and a one-man show. Welcome home,
son of Jamaica. Mel moved away when he was 10.

Drink white rum every afternoon with Parboosingh; artist elder,
we his fledglings. Everyone called him Parboo.

We learn to drive on the left, don't bite into Scotch Bonnets, ungarble the lilt
of patois, tuck in the mosquito net; how long to soak salt cod.

Step into dim-lit shacks with friend Martha, U.N. mental health counselor.
Children chained to beds, locked in sheds.

Uncles Eric and Colville invite us to Sunday dinners, regale us with
backyard breadfruit and mangos.

Dance with the Maroons high in the "cockpit" mountains. Come home
itching with grass lice.

We begin to notice only people with 'bright" skin and "good" hair
are the bank tellers, secretaries, on TV.

The color line tricks Mel, his blossoming Afro, blonde son, American
accent. Doors open a crack, then they close. "Lickle more."

Young Bob Marley lives up the street. Plays Rasta rallies in the park.
Woodsy smoke from spliffs fat as firecrackers; I Shot the Sheriff …

Black Pride a match striking a damp box. Only 10 years since Independence,
the girdle of British rule. Half the people

worship Haile Selassie, half wave tiny flags for the Queen.
Mel is not alone. Everyone's identity a jumble of jackstraws.

Prime Minister Manley pays the poor to hand-sweep streets.
Mel gets mural commission for the Bank of Jamaica.

We decide to stay.

Bus bumps and jars me to deep rural villages; I teach family planning
to 12-year-olds. They teach *me* a baby, the only dream they see.

Transfer our son from cane-switching, rote-teaching Mona Prep
to Priory, expat kids of execs, field trips and poetry.

Red-haired Scots and an Indian-Jamaican boy, our son's best friends.
Mel shows them how to catch lizards with a noose

of thread. I find comfort with other mixed-race couples, the most
we've ever known.

Mel represents Jamaica at FESTAC arts festival in Nigeria;
returns delirious with malaria.

OPEC oil embargo. Gas $5 a gallon, store shelves empty. U.S.
drivers line up at the pump, rant about the jump from 38¢ to 55.

We make cooking oil from coconuts, drain bacon on newspaper,
only cold water for dishes. The barefoot man

begs on our corner. I get free tuition
for a Masters at the University of the West Indies.

Bars on our windows. Squeeze a skull through,
any size body can get in. One does.

Our son sings in *Joseph and the Technicolor Dreamcoat.* Split
his brow slipping at a pool. ER orderly pins him down; stitches

with a re-used disposable needle. Mel gnaws curry-goat
on the beach with artists who can't afford canvas or paint.

Swills port on lawns with elite ones courting overseas buyers.
Art world politics contort, island-tight.

We find Parboo on the bathroom floor. Blood fountains
the walls, fingerpaints white tiles red. His profligate liver

burst; he dies, raging, in the ICU. Mel's work dries up.
I lose my job. Three weeks, sell all we can, land

in San Francisco. Local school, white kids bused in.
Our son's class is crowded, two years behind Priory.

We have no black friends.

Nancy L. Meyer

Waiting

Medium cold brew with a splash of oat:
her vocal fry is soft,
her eye bags made of crocheted wool,
strained at the handles.
Small Americano and a blueberry bagel,
please, toasted:
he's worn that sweater twice,
and it has a new hole near the wrist.
Iced caramel latte, medium, regular milk is fine:
this person is new,
a cash carrier, arrow tattoo on right index finger,
grey eyes the size of half dollars.
Order after order, matched, paired
with people etched into
the lunar dunes of my memory
whom I come to cherish …
trillions of iterations of unrequited love.
I never tire of waiting for eyes to notice me back.

AleX

Ghost

Everyone leaves.
I left you still carving
a pillar by the path we walked,
a monument to sorry,
a mask from stoic marble.

Is my name Ghost?
Dream hand reaches
toward your statuary brow
wanting to affront your eyes,
startle movement that cracks the facade.

You call me close but hold me
far off, using arts to lure,
engines and walls to contain.
The body bloats and swells to draw your eyes.
The soul stretches thin from reaching out.

Carolyn Ostrander

Only This, Just In

I once positioned my outpost on earth—
at the time, within earshot of owls
and a lake's short waves—
to be the center of all communication
beaming in from everywhere, out
to all the warped, rounded corners
of this universe. I was hoping
to fool that alien sense
I imagined as native to many,
that I was actually practically cut off
from the prime gist of being alive.
So, rather than scanning for more
koans-on-transcendence or
a how-to to convince the chipmunk
standing in for my mind
that this felt insignificance
was insignificant, thereby
skirting the issue that acted
as my Everest because
it was *there, it was always there!*—
I pitched a little white tent in a holler
with vents in the canvas to let in, let out
my antennae, the requisite wires,
and the million telekinetic messages
I'd be managing by the minute,
like some ancient eighty-armed operator
devotedly plugging in, plugging out,
the supple joint articulating a life to life.
And when all systems were finally go,
and after I flicked the little switch (a
Venetian-like light flooding the moon
of my face), the first words in were
wind, and how old leaves left alone
will crackle for no particular reason.

Then the slow creaking of tall beeches
followed by a pulsing, silent swooshing
as if I were holding my own personal shell
to my own individual ear,
which, naturally,
as was my custom,
I was.

D. R. James

Last Words

I live alone
with my guinea pig,
but she doesn't speak
and rarely squeaks.

Each day
I try to remember
the last words someone said to me
before I go home
to be alone,
for if I die,
these would be the last words
absorbed by my body
through my ears
and into my spirit.

I listen and note
that possible final blessing
to sing or poet me home.

See ya.
Have a good one.
Do you want me to lock this door?
This was a good day.
We can do it better next time.
Thank you.

If the words seem too distorted
for a send-off to eternity,
I stop on the way home
at the grocery store,
never using self-checkout.

Do you want a bag for that?
Have a nice day.
Want to round that up to feed the hungry?
Oh, you've got coupons.
You, too.

I always believe in
the worst-case scenario,
so I carry words as blessings
when they were only meant to be words.

I live alone.
I am afraid to die alone.
I am afraid to be dead alone.

May my final words not be, *Oh, shit,*
last words
absorbed by my body
through my ears
and into my spirit,
a final blessing for eternity.

Do you want a bag for that?
would be so much better

Teri Harroun

The Artist

His hands were the first thing I noticed—
large, powerful, scarred,
covered in stains. Chromatic hands
that had seen a life perilous.
He obviously lived on the street
or in some forgotten corner of a building
abandoned to despair or back taxes.

Beside him was a shabby backpack,
olive drab army surplus
with a duffel bag to match,
filled with a large roll of canvas
covered in paint. I realized with shock that he was a painter
and his hands were not grimed by life on the street
but coated in bright layers of oil paint
slightly muted by turpentine.

"What do you paint?" I asked.
His eyes looked like prisoners
caught in a cage before they focused on something
beyond his alley or the cityscape,
somewhere near the edge of things
that only he could see. His lips moved
without words, and his arms and hands
twitched and spasmed, then
swept in grand gestures
as if he were painting on the air.

Coming to himself, he looked down at his now stilled
hands as if he didn't recognize them.
"I paint what I see," he said simply, opening
the duffel and unfurling his canvas roll.

There were paintings obsessive with detail,
followed by abstract landscapes,
skies that melted into flowers,

and weightless stones that might be destined to fly.
I felt as if I breathed unimagined air,
as if I were empty canvas prepared for paint
and waiting to be brushed into existence.
"I would like to buy some of your paintings," I said.

I knew as soon as I'd said those words I had made a mistake.
The artist's eyes stared like stinging wasps, then tightly closed.
"Do you think you can buy my vision—steal my eyes?
Do you think you can buy the wind?"

He rolled up his canvas world and stuffed it in his duffel,
disappearing into the neon city and a vision
I knew I could not follow.

Patrick Kalahar

Interview with Hiromi Yoshida, winner of the Editor's Choice Award for Issue Eleven

Hiromi Yoshida is a first-generation Asian American poet. Born of a Japanese mother and Taiwanese father in Tokyo, she grew up within the four-block neighborhood of Columbia University before returning to Japan to attend the International School of the Sacred Heart in Tokyo. At ISSH, she served as co-editor of *The Green & Gold* school newspaper before graduating with distinction in English and art.

She returned to New York City to attend Fordham University, where she majored in English for a Bachelor of Arts degree and won a Presidential Scholarship toward a Master of Arts degree in English. While in NYC, she interned for *Opera News* Magazine and worked with activist Yuri Kochiyama.

She made another big move when she attended Indiana University, Bloomington, where she earned a second Master's degree, this time in library and information science. While studying for the degree, she curated *"The Big Strip Tease" of Sylvia Plath* exhibition at the Lilly Library. This exhibition curation experience inspired her Plath poems that have been published in *Last Stanza Poetry Journal, Plath Profiles,* and *Alien Buddha Zine,* and included in her Icarus poetry chapbooks.

Hiromi Yoshida is now an independent editing and writing professional and has contributed to *Bloom* Magazine, *Limestone Post, The Bloomingtonian, Ryder* Magazine, and *Video Librarian.* She also teaches poetry for the Indiana Writers Center while serving on the editorial boards for *Flying Island Journal, Plath Profiles,* and *Gidra* Magazine. A member of the Artistic Advisory Committee for Constellation Stage & Screen, she also serves as Literary Arts Representative for the Arts Alliance of Greater Bloomington and coordinates the Last Sunday Poetry & Open Mic program for the Writers Guild at Bloomington. She is the author of *Joyce & Jung: "The Four Stages of Eroticism" in A Portrait of the Artist as a Young Man,* and her poetry chapbooks are: *Icarus Burning, Epicanthus,* and *Icarus Redux.* Her *Icarus Superstar* and *Icarus Hieroglyph* chapbooks are forthcoming in 2023.

**Where are you living? Where were you raised?
Does that color your poetry?**

I currently reside in Bloomington, Indiana, and was raised in New York City and Tokyo, Japan. Definitely yes. Because my poems are rooted in all three places, they treat subjects and themes that are specific to them. For example, many of the poems in *Epicanthus* are about my childhood experiences in New York City and Tokyo, while those in my forthcoming *Icarus Superstar* chapbook are flashback snapshots of my young adult experiences in NYC. Bloomington-specific poems have been included in *Icarus Burning* and the INverse Poetry Archive.

**How long have you been writing creatively?
What prompted you to begin writing poetry?**

I'd say I began my full-time poetry writing career since graduating from IU Bloomington in 2015. So, that means I'm going on eight years since I've been writing poetry continuously. As for what prompted me to begin writing poetry .... It's difficult to pinpoint that exactly, since I began writing poems when I was about ten. Possibly, the poems that were embedded in the fairy tales within the Andrew Lang edited collections inspired me to try my hand at poems since that age. My early exposure to poetry might have been inspirational, as well, starting with Mother Goose's nursery rhymes and moving on to Robert Louis Stevenson's *A Child's Garden of Verses,* then Eugene Field's *Poems for Children* and Phyllis McGinley's edited collection, *Wonders and Surprises.*

Which is your personal favorite of your own poems?

My personal favorite is "Icarus Burning."

Excerpt:

... coin-sized overreach toward the numb vanishing point of
                          decimated dollars and decapitated cents.
And Icarus minted in accolades of green—
plunging into the copperplate sea of acidic tears—waxing toward the boiling point on the
Hudson horizon of disheveled trees in Riverside Park—
of sinking suns and new moons giving new birth to the fallen

stars and the debris of night, the harlot's jewelcase flung open
at the neon feet of commuters surging through turnstiles—
roiling mass of Nikes and rollerblades and Evian limbs
winging home on spiked Gatorade.
Deli lights splintering

through the fluorescent eyes of the nymphomaniac caravan
needling through the needy night murmurous with the junky scrawl of graffiti
incantations
rumbling through the groins of iconoclastic acolytes—

I'm particularly fond of the long lines and their musicality—also, the imagery that's densely packed into them. In fact, I've memorized this entire excerpt, plus more. Throughout this poem, Icarus is a subtext, a signifier of desire, "minted in accolades of green," as greening pennies materialize. The corporate greed of Wall Street, the sex addiction of Village hipsters, the desperation of subway beggars—all of these are also undercurrents within this New York City desire narrative tapestry. So, "Icarus Burning" is now readable as an expressionistic and surrealist overture, or prelude, to the poems in my forthcoming *Icarus Superstar* chapbook. These new poems elaborate on the more enigmatic lines of "Icarus Burning," unpacking that tapestry without unraveling it.

What is something surprising about yourself that may not be easily perceived through your writing?

Great question. Possibly, the fact that I had learned English through total immersion—and only after I had also done that with Japanese up until age three.

Do you have any advice for poets?

After receiving workshop feedback for your poems, consider returning to them much later—maybe even years later. That way, it's possible to approach them more objectively. And also, who knows? You might've moved beyond them by then. So, never throw out your workshopped drafts. They're valuable records of your growth as a poet.

Also, as Michael Salcman has advised in the previous *LSPJ* issue, read aloud your poems after their tentative completion. That way, it's easy to discern what works or doesn't work within that draft. For example, you might end up changing line breaks or adding, deleting, or substituting words or expressions. Either way, you'll make better editing decisions if you read aloud.

Good luck!

Adiela Akoo is a South African Poet, Author, and Founder of *The Quilled Ink Review* literary journal. She is a recipient of the prestigious DUX Award and was nominated as one of the Top Seven Most Promising Literary Influencers in the GBC Awards 2020, among others. She has represented the Durban UNESCO City of Literature in various collaborations with other cities of literature. Adiela has been published in a variety of anthologies and journals, including *Best of Africa, Best Emerging Poets of 2019, Best New African Poets of 2020* and *2022, The Penmen Review, Fidelities, Universul*  *Culturii, 25 Years of Freedom, ILA Magazine, OPA,* and others. Her poem "Whiplash" was quoted in The House of Parliament, and others have won poetry contests. *Lost in a Quatrain* is her debut collection. Her book was First Runner Up for poetry in the SAIP Awards 2021. Her second collection will launch in 2023. Connect with Adiela on social media @AdielaAkoo or @adiela_akoo on Instagram.

AleX is a budding poet from the cozy corners of East Texas and a physics major at Harvey Mudd College. She enjoys writing about the magic in the mundane.

David Allen is a retired journalist, sailor, and former poetry journal  producer and editor. He is also the host of the Freed Verse Society in Chesterfield, IN. He is a member and past vice president of the Poetry Society of Indiana. He has been published in numerous journals and anthologies, and has four books of poetry available from Amazon. Visit his webpage, Type Dancing, at davidallenpoet.net.

Amanda Anastasi is an Australian poet whose work has been published in *The Massachusetts Review, Griffith Review,* and *Best Australian Science Writing* 2021 and 2022. Amanda just completed a three-year poetry residency at the Monash Climate Change Communication Research Hub. Her latest poetry collection, *The Inheritors* (Black Pepper Publishing, 2021), explores the vulnerability of and deep connection between all living things.

Originally from England, **Linda Anderson** has lived in Perth, Western Australia since 1988. Way back in childhood, she dreamed of being a writer, but one day she realised she had been in Perth nearly half her life and hadn't even come close. As John Lennon famously said, "Life is what happens when you're busy making other plans." And where there were once vast oceans of time, now there was just a fast-running stream. Presently, she's busy trying to make some of those other plans come true. Her favourite poets range from Wyatt to Philip Larkin, but poetry, the sort that makes you catch your breath, is everywhere. Today, Leonard Cohen's "There is a crack in everything. That's how the light gets in," is as relevant and as revelatory as Shakespeare's "Shall I compare thee to a summer's day?"

Michael Ansara spent many years as an activist and an organizer starting with the civil rights movement of the 1960's, going on to be a regional organizer for SDS. He spent 10 years organizing opposition to the war in Vietnam. He was for 15 years a community organizer including directing Mass Fair Sharre. He has worked on political campaigns, coordinated voter registration efforts, and trained many organizers. He owned and ran two successful businesses. He is the co-founder of Mass Poetry. He currently serves on the Executive Committee of the Redress Movement and the organizing team for Together We Elect. His poems have appeared in numerous journals and his essays have appeared in *Vox, Arrowsmith, Solstice,* and *Cognoscenti.* He is currently working on a memoir. He lives in Carlisle, MA, with his wife, Barbara Arnold, and dotes on his three children and six grandchildren.

Lynn Axelrod's poetry has appeared in *California Quarterly, Medical Literary Messenger, Pendemic.ie* (Univ. College Dublin Special Collections), *Poetry Lovers' Daily Poem, Poetry X Hunger, The Avocet, Birdland Journal, Marin Poetry Center;* anthologized in *Freedom of New Beginnings: Poems of Witness And Vision* and *Pandemic Puzzle Poems* (invited), elsewhere, and featured in *The San Francisco Chronicle.*

Sarah Aziz is a poet, journalist, translator, and illustrator based in Kolkata, India. She is currently pursuing an undergraduate degree in English Literature at Loreto College, University of Calcutta. Her work appears or is forthcoming in *Voice of America, Mantis* (a Journal of Poetry, Criticism & Translation housed at Stanford University), and *The Lumiere Review,* among others.

Alex Barr's recent poetry is in *Poetry Review, The MacGuffin, Scintilla,* *The Dark Horse,* and *Orbis.* His poetry collections are *Letting in the Carnival* from Peterloo, *Henry's Bridge* from Starborn, and *Bedding Plants for My Father* from Cerasus. He is co-author of *Orchards,* a verse translation of Rilke's French poetry sequence *Vergers* published by Starborn. He lives in West Wales, where he organizes poetry workshops and readings.

Lois Baer Barr is a literacy tutor in Chicago and writes with Bluff Coast Writers. Thrice nominated for a Pushcart, Barr was a finalist for the Rita Dove Poetry Prize. Her chapbook *Tracks: Poems on the "L,"* a finalist in Finishing Line Press New Voices, Contest is available at www.finishinglinepress.com/product/tracks-poems-on-the-l-by-lois-baer-barr-nwvs-170

Marilyn J Baszczynski, originally from Ontario, Canada, lives and writes in rural Iowa. Her book, *Gyuri. A Poem of Wartime Hungary*, was published in 2015. Her poetry has appeared in the *TelepoemBooth Iowa* art installation and in anthologies and journals including *Abaton, Aurorean, Backchannels, Conestoga Zen, Gyroscope, Healing Muse, KYSO Flash, Last Stanza Poetry, Shot Glass Journal, Slippery Elm, Tipton Poetry Journal.* Marilyn is currently Editor of Iowa Poetry Association's annual anthology, *Lyrical Iowa.*

Roderick Bates edits Rat's Ass Review. His poems appear in *The Dark* *Horse, Stillwater Review, Naugatuck River Review, Cultural Weekly, Asses of Parnassus, fēlan, Three Line Poetry, Last Stanza Poetry Journal, Ekphrastic Review,* and *Anti-Heroin Chic,* among others. He also writes prose, and won an award from the International Regional

Magazines Association for an essay published in Vermont Life. He is a Dartmouth graduate and lives, writes, and edits in southern Vermont.

Les Bernstein's poems have appeared in journals, presses, and anthologies in the U.S.A. and internationally. Her chapbooks *Borderland, Naked Little Creatures*, and *Amid the Din* have been published by Finishing Line Press. Les is a winner of the 6th annual Nazim Hikmet Festival. She also was a Pushcart Prize Nominee for 2015. Les has been the editor of Redwood Writer's anthologies for the last five years and was the editor of the Marin High School Anthology 2018. Les' full length poetry book, *Loose Magic,* has been published by Finishing Line Press and is available on Amazon.

Charlie Brice won the 2020 Field Guide Poetry Magazine Poetry Contest and placed third in the 2021 Allen Ginsberg Poetry Prize. His sixth full-length poetry collection is *Pinnacles of Hope* (Impspired Books, 2022). His poetry has been nominated three times for both the Best of Net Anthology and the Pushcart Prize and has appeared in *Atlanta Review, The Honest Ulsterman, Ibbetson Street, The Paterson Literary Review, Impspired Magazine, Salamander Ink Magazine,* and elsewhere.

Michael Brockley is a retired school psychologist who lives in Muncie, Indiana where he is looking for a dog to adopt. His poems have appeared in *Syncopated Literary Journal, Shorts Magazine,* and *Jasper's Folly Poetry Journal.* Poems are forthcoming in *Gargoyle.*

Michael H. Brownstein's latest volumes of poetry, *A Slipknot to Somewhere Else* (2018) and *How Do We Create Love* (2019) were both published by Cholla Needles Press. In addition, he has appeared in *Skidrow Penthouse, Last Stanza Poetry Journal, American Letters and Commentary, Xavier Review, Hotel Amerika, Meridian Anthology of Contemporary Poetry, The Pacific Review,* Poetrysuperhighway.com, *Café Review,* and others. He has nine poetry chapbooks including *A Period of Trees* (Snark Press, 2004), *Firestorm: A Rendering of Torah* (Camel Saloon Press, 2012), *The Possibility of Sky and Hell: From My Suicide Book* (White Knuckle Press, 2013) and *The Katy Trail, Mid-Missouri, 100 Degrees Outside and Other Poems* (Kind of Hurricane Press, 2013). He is the editor of *First Poems from Viet Nam* (2011).

Melissa Cannon was born in New Hampshire and grew up in Tennessee. She has been writing for seven decades. Poetry has been her life's one continuous thread. She has published a chapbook, *Sister Fly Goes to Market,* and her poems have appeared in many small-press journals and anthologies. Five poems are forthcoming in an anthology from Querencia Press and five in *Sinister Wisdom's* issue "We Teach Sex to Everyone." She is currently working on a manuscript entitled *The Mortal Coil.*

Dan Carpenter is a freelance journalist, poet, fiction writer and essayist, born and residing in Indianapolis. He has published poems, stories and essays in *Last Stanza Poetry Journal, Poetry East, The Laurel Review, Illuminations, Pearl, Xavier Review, Fiction,* and many other journals. He has published two books of poems, *The Art He'd Sell for Love* (Cherry Grove) and *More Than I Could See* (Restoration); and two of non-fiction. He blogs at dancarpenterpoet.wordpress.com.

Kersten Christianson is a poet and English teacher from Sitka, Alaska. She has authored *Curating the House of Nostalgia* (Sheila-Na-Gig), *What Caught Raven's Eye* (Petroglyph Press), and *Something Yet to Be Named* (Kelsay Books). Kersten enjoys road trips, bookstores, and smooth ink pens.

Emma Conally-Barklem is a yogi, writer and poet based in Yorkshire, England. Her poetry has been published in *Free Verse Revolution Literary*  *Magazine, Black in White Community Collection Anthology, Please See Me Online Literary Journal, Aurum Journal, Sunday Mornings at The River, Ey Up! Bent Key Publishing Summer Anthology, Tipping the Scales Literary Journal, Small Leaf Press, Super Present Magazine, Harvest Anthology QuillKeepers Press, West Trestle Review, Querencia Press, Black Cat Poetry Press* and *Wild Roof Journal.* Pushcart Prize nominated, Emma had a summer residency at the Bronte Parsonage Museum and was named one of Ilkley Poetry Festival's New Northern Poets 2022. She was featured on BBC Radio York where she was interviewed and performed her poem "Magoa." Her first collection, *The Ridings* was accepted for traditional chapbook publication by *Bent Key Publishing* in March 2023. Her yoga and grief memoir, *You Can't Hug A Butterfly: Love, Loss & Yoga* was accepted for traditional publication by QuillKeepers Press in 2024.

Melinda Coppola writes from a messy desk in small town Massachusetts, where her four cats often monitor her progress. She delights in mothering her complicated, enchanting daughter who defies easy description. Melinda's work has appeared in many fine books and publications, most recently *One Art, Third Wednesday,* and *Thimble.*

San Francisco poet **Kitty Costello**'s collection *Upon Waking: New & Selected Poems 1977-2017* was released in 2018. She is coeditor of the anthology *Muslim American Writers at Home: Stories, Essays & Poems of Identity, Diversity & Belonging,* 2021. She is literary executor for indigenous Alaskan writer Mary TallMountain, and she serves on the editorial board of Freedom Voices Publications, whose mission is to publish works that speak to and from communities on the margins.

 Ryan Cresswell is a Cape Town based journalist who has worked in Southern Africa and Canada. He has had a range of content published, from short stories and poetry to satirical columns and business editorials. Ryan has had a lifelong interest in literature, travel, history and politics. He holds a BA Hons in the History of the Ancient Near East.

Say Davenport grew up running through the woods, finding magic in absolutely everything. At University, she studied cultures and religion because she's fascinated by the world and what people find in it that makes it have meaning for them. She is a  writer, educator, big dog lover, and avid traveler who seeks adventure wherever she can, either out in the world or between the pages of a book. As a writer, she takes inspiration from the idea that a person should write what they want to read and, for her, that usually means magic and salt.

Dr. Vivian Delchamps is an Assistant Professor of English at Dominican University of California. She received her B.A. in English with minors in French and Dance at Scripps College (2014). She received her M.A. (2017) and Ph.D. (2022) in English at the University of California, Los Angeles. Delchamps primarily researches and teaches the politics of diagnosis and entanglements of disability, gender, and race in American literature. She is also a dancer and poet who writes about embodiment and chronic illness. Her favorite symbol is the ampers&.

Steve Denehan lives in Kildare, Ireland with his wife Eimear and daughter Robin. He is the author of two chapbooks and four poetry collections. Winner of the Anthony Cronin Poetry Award and twice winner of *Irish Times'* New Irish Writing, his numerous publication credits include *Poetry Ireland Review* and *Westerly.*

RC deWinter's poetry is widely anthologized, notably in *New York City Haiku* (NY Times, 2/2017), *easing the edges: a collection of everyday*  *miracles,* (Patrick Heath Public Library of Boerne, 11/2021) *The Connecticut Shakespeare Festival Anthology* (River Bend Bookshop Press, 12/2021), in print: *2River, Event, Gargoyle Magazine, the minnesota review, Night Picnic Journal, Plainsongs, Poetry South, Prairie Schooner, Southword, The Ogham Stone, Twelve Mile Review, Variant Literature,* and *York Literary Review* among many others and appears in numerous online literary journals.

Kathryn Dohrmann taught for many years in the Psychology and Environmental Studies Departments at a small college near Chicago. Her poems have been published in a variety of periodicals, including *CALYX, The Chicago Tribune, The A-3 Review, Thema, The Ekphrastic Review, The Last Stanza Poetry Journal, Turning Wheel: The Journal of the Buddhist Peace Fellowship,* and *Collaborative Visions: The Poetic Dialogue Project.* She writes with the Bluff Coast Writers.

Phoebe Eisenbeis is a writer, artist, and farmer living in Minnesota. She holds a B.A. from Lawrence University, where she studied English and Environmental Studies. She has worked on small farms in Minnesota, Wisconsin, and New York, which informs her writing and art.

Among **Karl Elder**'s honors are the Christopher Latham Sholes Award from the Council for Wisconsin Writers; a Pushcart Prize; the Chad Walsh, Lorine Niedecker, and Lucien Stryk Awards; and two appearances in *The Best American Poetry.* His novel, *Earth as It Is in Heaven,* is from Pebblebrook Press. Both *Alpha Images: Poems Selected and New* (Water's Edge Press) and *Reverie's Ilk: Collected Prose*

Poems (Cyberwit) appeared in 2020. *Random Acts* (Cyberwit), Elder's thirteenth volume, was released in June of 2022.

Thomas Ferrebee lives and works in Chile where he enjoys his work as an educator helping others become writers. He can be found with Leah and their two children seeking novelty living abroad and dreaming of some year in the future when they might get the itch to settle down back in the United States.

Meg Freer grew up in Montana and lives in Ontario. She enjoys the outdoors year-round and works as an editor and piano teacher. She has two poetry chapbooks out: *Serve the Sorrowing World* with Joy (Woodpecker Lane Press, 2020) and *A Man of Integrity* (Alien Buddha Press, 2022). Her photos, poetry, and prose have been published in anthologies and journals such as *Arc Poetry, Rat's Ass Review, The Sunlight Press, Eastern Iowa Review, Sequestrum,* and *Ruminate.*

The poetry of **David Lee Garrison** has been read by Garrison Keillor on "The Writer's Almanac" and featured by Ted Kooser in his column, "American Life in Poetry." Named Ohio Poet of the Year in 2014, his most recent book is *Light in the River* (Dos Madres Press).

Frances Gaudiano is the author of a book and many articles relating to veterinary science. Her novel, *The Listener,* was published in 2021 by Veneficia Press. She has been a veterinary nurse for nearly thirty years. She earned an M.A. in Dramatic Literature from the University of California at Santa Barbara and worked in theatre as a stage manager in England, California and Indonesia. She lives in Cornwall, England—a beautiful, dramatic place, but where there are very few cacti.

Lorraine Gibson is a Scottish-Australian writer, poet, and anthropologist living on Biripi country. Her recent and forthcoming poetry can be found at: *Meniscus Literary Journal, Eureka Street, Backstory, Hecate, Poetry for The Planet* (anthology), *Booranga FourW, Book of Matches, Burrow, Live Encounters, The Galway Review, Tarot, Writing in A Woman's Voice,* and *Lothlorien Poetry Journal.* Lorraine is author of, *We Don't Do Dots: Art and Culture in Wilcannia NSW,* Sean Kingston Press: Canon Pyon, UK.

Cosmo Goldsmith is a semi-retired English and Drama teacher who has worked in equal measures in the UK and Greece and still divides his time between the two countries. He enjoys all forms of creative writing and has had some poems and two short stories published.

James Green is a retired university professor and administrator. He has published five chapbooks of poetry and individual poems have appeared in literary journals in Ireland, the UK, and the USA.  His previous works have been nominated for a Pushcart Prize, Best of the Net and the Modern Language Association Conference on Christianity Book of the Year; and, his chapbook titled *Long Journey Home: Poems on Classical Myths* won the Charles Dickson Prize sponsored by the Georgia Poetry Society. His website can be found at www.jamesgreenpoetry.net.

John D. Groppe, Professor Emeritus at Saint Joseph's College,  Rensselaer, IN, has published in *Tipton Poetry Journal, Flying Island, From the Edge of the Prairie, Christianity Today, The National Catholic Reporter,* and other journals. His poem "A Prophet Came to Town" was nominated for a Pushcart Prize (2013), as was his poem "Caravaggio, Master of Luminosity" (2022). His poem "Sudden Death" won honorable mention in Embers poetry contest (1984). His poetry collection *The Raid of the Grackles and Other Poems* (Iroquois River Press) was published in 2016. He is listed on the Indiana Bicentennial Literary Map 200 Years: 200 Writers.

Gary Grossman is Professor Emeritus of Animal Ecology at University of Georgia. His poetry has been published in 30+ literary reviews. Short fiction in MacQueen's Quinterly and creative non-fiction in Tamarind Literary Magazine. Gary's micro-fiction piece "Mindfulness" was just nominated by MacQueen's Quinterly for inclusion in The Best Small Fictions Anthology 2022. For 10 years he wrote the "Ask Dr. Trout" column for American Angler. Gary's first book of poems, *Lyrical Years* is forthcoming in 2023 from Kelsay Press, and his graphic novel My Life in Fish: One Scientist's Journey is available from todaysecologicalsolutions@gmail.com Find him at garygrossman.net and garydavidgrossman.medium.com

Cynthia T. Hahn's poetic work includes two volumes of poetry, *Outside-In-Sideout*, Finishing Line Press, 2010, and *Coïncidence(s),* self-translated in French and English in collaboration with artist Monique Loubet, alfAbarre Press, Paris, 2014). She is a member of the Bluff Coast Writers and Highland Park Poets, and has been a professor of French, creative writing, and translation at Lake Forest College since 1990. Musical rhythms and visual art inspire her writing.

Teri Harroun is a gluten-free gummy-bear loving poet, parent, and priest. She serves as pastor at Light of Christ in Longmont, Colorado where she has also been named the church's poet laureate. Teri enjoys reading, crocheting, walking, and moose-ology (all the things you learn about God when you get yourself caught between a mama moose and her babies). She has one published  book of poetry: *A Woman Called Father: Reflections of Priesthood in a Woman's Body.*

Marc Harshman's *Woman in Red Anorak*, Blue Lynx Prize winner, was published in 2018 by Lynx House Press. His fourteenth children's book, *Fallingwater…*, co-author, Anna Smucker, was published by Roaring Brook/Macmillan and named an Amazon Book of the Month. He is co-winner of the 2019 Allen Ginsberg Poetry Award and his poem, "Dispatch from the Mountain State," was printed in 2020 Thanksgiving edition of *The New York Times*. Poems have been anthologized by Kent State University, the University of Iowa, University of Georgia, and the University of Arizona. Appointed in 2012, he is the seventh poet laureate of West Virginia and a native Hoosier.

Chris Hasara is a truck driver and farmer in Northern Indiana, writing as life and time allow. His printed words have appeared in *From the Edge of the Prairie, Last Stanza Poetry Journal,* and *Ink to Paper* volume 6. He can be heard reading his own work on an episode of *The Storyworks Podcast.*

Katherine Heil is a Michigan writer who can be found writing anything she likes and listening to music at every waking moment. With a fondness for books that she can read in a flash, she is currently getting into mystery novels.

John R. Hinton is an Indiana poet and writer. His writing is inspired by our daily human interactions and the accompanying emotions: love, hate, indifference, passion. His words explore who we are, how we behave. Sometimes eloquent, other times gritty, these words seek to reveal the joy and pain of living this beautiful human existence. He is the author of two poetry collections: *Blackbird Songs* and  *Held.* John is the President of the Poetry Society of Indiana and a member of Last Stanza Poetry Association.

Kaela Hinton is an aspiring writer from Indiana that finds inspiration in the world around her, especially mental health. She works with children on the spectrum for a living and is expecting her first child in January of this year.

Recently retired from nearly 40 years of teaching college writing, literature, and peace studies, **D. R. James** lives, writes, vegges, and cycles with his psychotherapist wife in the woods near Saugatuck, Michigan. His latest of ten collections are *Mobius Trip* and *Flip Requiem* (Dos Madres Press, 2021, 2020), and his prose and poems have appeared in a wide variety of print and online anthologies and journals. www.amazon.com/author/drjamesauthorpage

David James has published seven books; his most recent is *Alive in Your Skin While You Still Own It*, 2022. More than thirty of his one-act plays have been produced in the U.S. and Ireland.

Lily Jarman-Reisch's poems appear or are forthcoming in *CALYX Journal, Collateral, 3rd Wednesday, Fourth River, Light, Mediterranean*  *Poetry, Mobius, MONO, Rise Up Review, Route 7 Review, Snapdragon, The Military Review, Gleam, 1807, The Dewdrop,* and other international literary journals. She is a 2023 Pushcart Prize and Best of the Net nominee and poetry reviewer for *The Los Angeles Review.* She has been a journalist in Washington, D.C., and Athens, Greece, where she lived aboard a small boat she sailed throughout the Aegean and Ionian. She has also held administrative and teaching positions at the Universities of Michigan and Maryland, sailed across the Atlantic, and hiked on four continents.

Lorraine Jeffery has won numerous prizes and published many poems in journals including *Clockhouse, Canary, Rockhurst Review, Naugatuck River Review, Orchard Street, Two Hawks,* and *Bacopa Press.* Her first book is titled *When the Universe Brings Us Back,* 2022, and her chapbook titled *Tethers,* published by Kelsay Books, is forthcoming.

Jenny Kalahar (Poetry Society of Indiana's Premier Poet for 2022-2025) is the editor and publisher of *Last Stanza Poetry Journal.* She is the

founding leader of Last Stanza Poetry Association in Elwood, Indiana. Jenny and her husband, poet Patrick, are used and rare booksellers. She was the humor columnist for *Tails Magazine* for several years and the treasurer for Poetry Society of Indiana. Author of fifteen books, she was twice nominated for a Pushcart Prize and once for Best of the Net. Her poems have been published in journals, anthologies, and newspapers. Her works can be found on poemhunter.com and *INverse,* Indiana's poetry archive. She will have a poem on the moon via a NASA launch in 2024 as part of the *Polaris Trilogy* from Brick Street Poetry. Through Stackfreed Press, she has published books for numerous authors. Contact her at laststanza@outlook.com

Patrick Kalahar is a used and rare bookseller with his wife, Jenny, and a book conservationist. He is a veteran, world traveler, avid reader, and book collector. He is a member of Last Stanza Poetry Association. His poems have been published in *Tipton Poetry Journal, Flying Island, Rail Lines, The Moon and Humans, Polk Street Review, Northwest Indiana Literary Journal,* and *A Disconsolate Planet.*

Patrick can be seen as an interviewee in the Emmy-winning documentary *James Whitcomb Riley: Hoosier Poet,* and he gives costumed and scholarly readings as Edgar Allan Poe.

James Kangas is a retired librarian and musician living in Flint, Michigan. His poems have appeared in *Atlanta Review, Faultline, The New York Quarterly, The Penn Review, Unbroken, West Branch,* et al. His chapbook, *Breath of Eden* (Sibling Rivalry Press), was published in 2019.

Former Indiana Poet Laureate **Norbert Krapf**'s fifteenth collection, *Spirit Sister Dance*, about his stillborn sister (Jan. 25, 1950) was released in late October. You can read about it at www.krapfpoetry.net. His *Homecomings: A Writer's Memoir*, which covers the fifty plus years of his writing and publishing life, will come out in spring, 2023.

Wayne Lee (wayneleepoet.com) lives in Santa Fe, NM. Lee's poems have appeared in *Pontoon, Slipstream, The New Guard, The Lowestoft Chronicle,* and other journals and anthologies. He was awarded the 2012 Fischer Prize and has been nominated for a Pushcart Prize and three Best of the Net Awards. His collection *The Underside of Light* was a finalist for the 2014 New Mexico/Arizona Book Award. He is currently working on a full-length collection called *Dining on Salt: Four Seasons of Septets* and a memoir, *Service Husband: A Caregiver's Journey Through Disability, Suicide & Recovery.*

Stella Ling writes: Life is a feast; we celebrate this feast with poetry. Before I write it, I visualize it, smell it, jump in it, kiss it, then rip it free. I run the Wilmington Writers Collaborative which is available to anyone to join via zoom; we meet quarterly now, and you are please invited. I live in Ohio, California, and Hawaii by turns, and travel the world if and when free.

Native New Yorker **LindaAnn LoSchiavo**, a Pushcart Prize, Rhysling Award, Best of the Net, and Dwarf Stars nominee, is a member of SFPA, The British Fantasy Society, and The Dramatists Guild. Elgin Award winner *A Route Obscure and Lonely, Concupiscent Consumption, Women Who Were Warned,* Firecracker Award, Balcones Poetry Prize, and IPPY Award nominee *Messengers of the Macabre* [co-written with David Davies], *Apprenticed to the Night* [Beacon Books, 2023], and *Felones De Se: Poems about Suicide* [Ukiyoto Publishing, 2023] are her  latest poetry titles. Twitter: @Mae_WestsideLindaAnn Literary: www.youtube.com/channel/UCHm1NZIlTZybLTFA44wwdfg

Carolyn Martin is a lover of gardening and snorkeling, feral cats and backyard birds, writing and photography. Her poems have appeared in more than 175 journals throughout North America, Australia, and the UK. Find out more at carolynmartinpoet.com.

Herbert Woodward Martin has published eleven volumes of poems. His  most recent success has been in the writing of libretti and *A Knee on The Neck*, composed by American Adolphus Hailstork. This was his fifth venture in the realm of music, if such a distinction should be made. His sixth libretti is titled *Ukrainian Songs*, and has been set by the American composer Steven Winteregg. His imagination is being tempted by the Emmett Till story.

Kate Maxwell is a teacher and writer from Sydney. She's been published and awarded in many Australian and International literary magazines. Her first poetry anthology, *Never Good at Maths (IP Press)*, was published in 2021 and her second anthology *(Ginninderra Press)* is forthcoming in 2023. Her interests include film, wine, and sleeping. She can be found at kateswritingplace.com

Jill McGrath is a Seattle poet who loves outdoor adventures like biking and hiking, and indoor adventures on the dance floor. Memorable escapades include a two-year journey in Asia on a tandem bicycle and a one-year stint editing tourism magazines in Nepal. She is currently editing a poetry manuscript based on bicycle travels in Asia, and she is circulating a first book for publication. She's published a chapbook, *The Rune of Salt Air*, and she has also had forty-five poems published in literary magazines, including *the Seattle Review, The MacGuffin, Southern Poetry Review, West Wind Review*, and *Poet & Critic*.

Linda McQuarrie-Bowerman lives in Lake Tabourie, NSW, Australia. She's written most of her poetry since 2021and is completing her Degree in Creative Writing at Curtin University. She has so far been published on Viewlesswings.com, in *The Ekphrastic Review, Right Hand Pointing, One Sentence Poems (OSP), the Star 82 Review, Cathexis Northwest Press*, with work forthcoming in *Misfit*, and two pieces selected for *Brushstrokes*, the 2022 Ros Spencer Poetry Award Anthology. Another two poems are to be published in the South Coast Writers Centre Digital Anthology, *Coast*. Her poem "Shiver" has been nominated by the *Star 82 Review* for Best Spiritual Literature, formerly the *Orison Anthology*. She recently branched into flash fiction, and her first piece was short-listed for the 2022 Berry Writers Festival Award. Her poem "Wakizashi" has been nominated for the 2023 Pushcart Prize.

Stephen Mead is an Outsider multi-media artist and writer. Since the 1990s, he's been grateful to many editors for publishing his work in print zines and eventually online. He is also grateful to have managed to keep various day jobs for the Health Insurance. Recent publications include *Swifts & Slows, Visibility Magazine,* and *Tourniquet.* Currently he is resident artist/curator for The Chroma Museum, artistic  renderings of LGBTQI historical figures, organizations, and allies predominantly before Stonewall. https://thestephenmeadchromamuseum. weebly.com/

 **Nancy L. Meyer** she/her is a 2020 Pushcart nominee, avid cyclist, grandmother of five from the unceded Ramaytush Ohlone lands of San Francisco. Recent journals include: *Feral Journal, Third Prize Nebraska Poetry Society Open Contest, New Note, Outcast, Gyroscope, BeZine, Book of Matches, Laurel Review, Sugar House Review.* Forthcoming: *International Human Rights Arts Festival, Decolonial Passage, Kind of a Hurricane Press, Frost Meadow, Black Moon Poetry.* In eight anthologies, including by Tupelo Press, Ageless Authors and Wising Up Press.

David P. Miller's collection, *Bend in the Stair,* was published by Lily Poetry Review Books in 2021. *Sprawled Asleep* was published by Nixes Mate Books in 2019. Poems have recently appeared in *Meat for Tea, Hawaii Pacific Review, Turtle Island Quarterly, Clementine Unbound, Constellations, J Journal, The Lily Poetry Review, Ibbetson Street, Redheaded Stepchild, The Blue Pages,* and *What Rough Beast,* among others. His poem "Add One Father to Earth" was awarded an Honorable Mention by Robert Pinsky for the New England Poetry Club's 2019 Samuel Washington Allen Prize competition. He was a librarian at Curry College in Massachusetts, from which he retired in June 2018.

During a career practicing and teaching at UCLA's Department of Psychiatry, **W. Hans Miller** published three books: *Personal Stress Management for Medical Patients, Systematic Parent Training,* and a memoir, *Soothing: Lives of a Child Psychologist.* His poems appear in or are currently forthcoming in *Last Leaves, Last Stanza,* and several anthologies from the Moonstone Poetry Center including *Haiku 2022, HOPE 2022, Nonsense Verse,* and *Struggling for Liberty.* He has recently published my first book of poems, *Nancy's Song: 21 Poems* and a collection of poems *Mood and Memories of a Pilgrim* is currently in publication. His chapbook *Ever the End of Things* is forthcoming from the Moonstone Poetry Center.

David Milley has written and published since the 1970s, while working as a technical writer and web applications developer. His work has appeared in *Painted Bride Quarterly, Bay Windows, Friends Journal, RFD,* and *Capsule Stories.* Retired now, David lives in southern New Jersey with his husband and partner of forty-six years, Warren Davy, who's made his living as a farmer, woodcutter, nurseryman, auctioneer, beekeeper, and cook. These days, Warren tends his garden and keeps honeybees. David walks and writes.

Richard Moore is a native of Nottingham, UK. He's been writing short stories and novellas for quite some time, and has a story forthcoming in *The Passager Journal.* More recently, he's also been writing poetry which he puts down to the pandemic and being locked away for months. "Sandcastles Without Children" is his first published poem.

James B. Nicola is a returning contributor to *Last Stanza.* The latest of his seven full-length poetry collections (2014-22) are *Fires of Heaven: Poems of Faith and Sense* and *Turns & Twists.* Decades of working in the theater culminated in his nonfiction book *Playing the Audience: The Practical Guide to Live Performance,* which won a *Choice* award. A graduate of Yale University (BA cum laude, distinction in music), he currently hosts the Hell's Kitchen International Writers' Round Table at his library branch in Manhattan: walk-ins welcome.

James Nolan's latest book of poetry is *Nasty Water: Collected New Orleans Poems* (University of Louisiana at Lafayette Press, 2018). Previous collections are *Why I Live in the Forest, What Moves Is Not the Wind,* and *Drunk on Salt,* and his translations include volumes of  Neruda and Gil de Biedma. His *Flight Risk* won the 2018 Next-Generation Indie Book Award for Best Memoir. The three books of his fiction have been awarded a Faulkner-Wisdom Gold Medal, an Independent Publishers Book Award, and a Next-Generation Indie Book Award. The recipient of an NEA and two Fulbright fellowships, he has taught at universities in San Francisco, Florida, Barcelona, Madrid, Beijing, as well as in his native New Orleans. www.pw.org/directory/writers/james_nolan

Lylanne Musselman is an award-winning poet, playwright, and visual  artist. Her work has appeared in *Last Stanza Poetry Journal, Tipton Poetry Journal, The Indianapolis Review,* and *The Ekphrastic Review,* among many others, in addition to many anthologies. She is author of six chapbooks, and her seventh, *Staring Dementia in the Face* is forthcoming from Finishing Line Press. Musselman is author of the full-length poetry collection, *It's Not Love, Unfortunately* (Chatter House Press, 2018). A four-time Pushcart Prize nominee, her poems are included in the INverse Poetry Archive, a collection of Hoosier poets, housed at the Indiana State Library. Musselman is the director of the Blackford County Arts Center.

James B. Nicola is a returning contributor to *Last Stanza.* The latest of his seven full-length poetry collections (2014-22) are *Fires of Heaven: Poems of Faith and Sense* and *Turns & Twists.* Decades of working in the theater culminated in his nonfiction book *Playing the Audience: The Practical Guide to Live Performance,* which won a *Choice* award. A graduate of Yale  University (BA cum laude, distinction in music), he currently hosts the Hell's Kitchen International Writers' Round Table at his library branch in Manhattan: walk-ins welcome.

Carolyn Ostrander (she/they) lives and works in Central New York, in the unceded territory of the Haudenosaunee. Poems have previously appeared in or have been accepted by *Beyond Words, The Comstock Review*, and *Amethyst Review.*

Donna Pucciani was born in Washington, DC, grew up in New Jersey,  graduated magna cum laude from Marywood University with a degree in music, and earned an M.A. and Ph.D. in Humanities from New York University. She taught in secondary schools and colleges in the East and Midwest for several decades. Her poems have been published on four continents, translated into Chinese, Japanese, Italian and German, and nominated half a dozen times for the Pushcart Prize. She has won awards from the Illinois Arts Council, the National Federation of State Poetry Societies, Poetry on the Lake, and other organizations. A resident of the Chicago area, she served for many years as Vice President of the Poets Club of Chicago. Her latest book of poetry is *Edges*. (donnapuccianipoet.wordpress.com)

Royal Rhodes has had poems published recently in *The Lyric, Last Stanza, Plumtree Tavern, Abandoned Mine,* and *Lighten Up,* among other literary journals. Royal team-taught an interdisciplinary course on the Shoah for many years. His collaborative art and poetry exhibition, Specimens and Reflections, has been on view at the Fairfield University Art Gallery. He has been named the Poet Laureate of the Village in which he resides.

Recent work by **Bruce Robinson** appears or is forthcoming in *Tar River* *Poetry, Spoon River, Rattle, Mantis, Two Hawks Quarterly, Peregrine, Tipton Poetry Journal, North Dakota Quarterly, The Poetry Box,* and *Aji*. He divides his time uncertainly between Brooklyn and Albany, NY, as do, though not without protest, several four-footed and sure-footed animals.

For over 25 years, **Mimi Rosenbush** worked in film and television production in Chicago, including in film editing, documentary filmmaking, and co-directing the Midwest Region for Steven Spielberg's Shoah Foundation and working at Harpo on Oprah's Book Club team. Mimi then made a career pivot and taught grammar and English Composition at the University of Illinois at Chicago for ten years. In retirement, she has focused on writing creative non-fiction and, more recently, poetry. Her writing work, as well as her photography, can be viewed on her website: mimirosenbush.com.

Jen Ross is a Chilean-Canadian journalist and storyteller with more than 10 years on staff at the United Nations. In 2016, she took a sabbatical and moved to Aruba to write her first fiction and poetry. She decided to stay, and is now a university lecturer, writer, and editor. Her creative nonfiction has appeared in *Guernica Magazine*; her poetry in *The Poet Magazine, Better than Starbucks, the other side of hope,* and *Descant* (forthcoming); her short stories in *Pine Cone Review, Global Youth Review, Evocations Review* and *Isele Magazine* (forthcoming) and she has a novella published in the *Everlast* anthology by Dragon Soul Press.

Diane G. Scholl is Professor Emerita of English at Luther College in Decorah, Iowa, where she's taught American and modern British  literature, poetry courses, and literature by women. Her poems have been published by *Louisville Review, Cider Press Review, Sow's Ear Poetry Review, Cold Mountain Review, Spoon River Poetry Review,* and *Ruminate,* among other places. In 2019, her chapbook, *Salt,* was published by Seven Kitchens Press. When she's not writing, she enjoys hiking and biking among the scenic bluffs of NE Iowa and reading mysteries, a poet's food.

Mary Sexson is author of the award-winning book, *103 in the Light, Selected Poems 1996-2000* (Restoration Press), and co-author of *Company of Women, New and Selected Poems* (Chatter House Press). Her poetry has appeared in *Tipton Poetry Journal, Lion's Den Press, Laureate, Hoosier Lit, Flying Island, New Verse News, Grasslands Review,* and *Last Stanza Poetry Journal,* among others. She has recent work in *Reflections on Little Eagle Creek, Anti-Heroin Chic,* and *Last Stanza Poetry Journal* Issue #10. Sexson's newest work appears in *The Indianapolis Review* (November 2022). Finishing Line Press will publish her manuscript, *Her Addiction, An Empty Place at the Table,* in 2023. Sexson's poetry is part of the INverse Poetry Archives for Hoosier Poets. She has three Pushcart Prize nominations.

Sherry Shahan is a septuagenarian who lives in a laid-back beach town in California where she grows potatoes in the box that delivered a stereo. Her work has appeared in *Rattle, Exposition Review, ZYZZYVA, Critical Read, Oxford University Press,* and elsewhere. She earned an MFA from Vermont College of Fine Arts and taught a creative writing course for UCLA for ten years.

Robert Simon holds the title of Professor of Spanish and Portuguese at Kennesaw State University. Along with his numerous academic publications, he has also published ten collections of poetry, including *Ode to Friendship* (2021), for which he was nominated for the Georgia Writers Association Author of the Year Award in 2022, *The Bridge* (2019), and *The Musician* (2017), as well as with poems in various journals in India, Portugal, and the United States. He enjoys reading, running, spending time with his daughter, and playing the oboe.

Maximilian Speicher (www.maxspeicher.com) is a designer who writes, mostly sitting on his balcony in Barcelona, watching his orange trees grow. Although he's been writing poetry on and off for many years, he only recently started submitting it. His first published poems have appeared in *Impspired*, and more are forthcoming in *Otoliths Magazine* and *The Avalon Literary Review*.

Margaret D. Stetz is the Mae & Robert Carter Professor of Women's Studies and Professor of Humanities at the University of Delaware, where she teaches courses that reflect the intersection of the arts. Recently, her poetry has appeared in *A Plate of Pandemic, C*nsorship Magazine, Kerning, Mono, Review Americana, Rushing Thru the Dark, West Trestle Review, Existere, Hare's Paw, Azure,* and other journals, as well as in the *Washington Post*.

Michael E. Strosahl grew up blocks from the Mississippi, pulled his roots and moved to Indiana, where he discovered the Indianapolis poetry scene, participating in many groups around the state, including Last Stanza. In addition to regularly submitting to this journal, his work appears often in the *Tipton Poetry Journal* and in a weekly blogspot post he does for the site Moristotle & Company. He currently resides between two rivers in Jefferson City, Missouri.

Connie S. Tettenborn, PhD, began a career as a scientist in biotechnology and then transitioned to scientific editing and poetry, which includes visual and mathematical poetry created using watercolor or digital media. In addition to *Last Stanza Poetry Journal*, her poetry has appeared in the *Deronda Review* and *California Quarterly,* among others, as well as various online venues such as *Farmer-ish* and *The Piker Press.* She currently lives in the San Francisco Bay Area.

Rp Verlaine lives in New York City. He has an MFA in creative writing  from City College. He taught in New York Public schools for many years. His first volume of poetry, *Damaged by Dames & Drinking,* was published in 2017, and another, *Femme Fatales Movie Starlets & Rockers,* in 2018. A set of three e-books titled *Lies from The Autobiography vol 1-3* were published from 2018 to 2020. His newest book, *Imagined Indecencies,* was published in February of 2022. He was nominated for a pushcart prize in poetry in 2021 and 2022.

Winner of The Writers' Union of Canada's 2016 short prose contest, **Susan Wadds'** short fiction and poetry have been featured in literary journals and anthologies, including *The Blood Pudding, Room, Quagmire,* and *carte blanche* magazines. The first two chapters of her forthcoming novel, "What the Living Do," won  Lazuli Literary Group's writing contest, and were published in *Azure*'s winter 2017 issue. "What the Living Do" is set for a 2024 release by Regal House Publishing. A graduate of the Humber School for Writers, Susan is certified in the Amherst Writers and Artists (AWA) method of writing workshop facilitation.

J.T. Whitehead earned a law degree from Indiana University, *Bloomington.* He received a master's degree in Philosophy from Purdue, where he studied Existentialism, social and political philosophy, and Eastern Philosophy. He spent time between, during, and after schools on a grounds crew, as a pub cook, a writing tutor, a teacher's assistant, a delivery man, a book shop clerk, and a liquor store clerk, inspiring four years as a labor lawyer on the workers' side. Whitehead was Editor in Chief of *So It Goes: The Literary Journal of the Kurt Vonnegut Memorial Library,* briefly, for issues 1, 2, 3, 4, and 6. He is a *Pushcart Prize*-nominated short story author, a *Pushcart Prize*-nominated poet, and was winner of the *Margaret Randall Poetry Prize* in 2015 (published in *Mas Tequila Review*). Whitehead has published over 315 poems in over 120 literary journals, including *The Lilliput Review*, *Slipstream*, *Left Curve*, *The Broadkill Review*, *The Blue Collar Review*, *Home Planet News*, *The Iconoclast*, *Poetry Hotel*, *Last Stanza*, *Book XI*, and *Gargoyle*. His book *The Table of the Elements* was nominated for the *National Book Award* in 2015. Whitehead lives in Indianapolis with his two sons, Daniel and Joseph.

Dr. Thomas Reed Willemain is a former academic, software entrepreneur, and intelligence officer. A graduate of Princeton and MIT, his poetry has appeared in *Autumn Sky Poetry, Two Thirds North, Idle Ink, Dillydoun Review,* and elsewhere. A native of western Massachusetts, Tom lives with his wife near the Mohawk River in upstate New York.

Emmanuel Williams is an Englishman living in the Sierra foothills of East California. He worked as a teacher all over the world. He was a teacher who wrote. Now 84, he's a writer who occasionally teaches. He has self-published books on Amazon. His poetry has been published in a number of magazines.

Christy Wise is a poet, essayist and author. Her poems have appeared in *Panoplyzine, Anthem,* and *Upside Down and From Below: Marin Poetry Center Anthology 2022,* among others. Her poem, "Last Day of Prophecy Season" was a finalist in the San Francisco Writers Contest. Christy is co-author of *A Mouthful of Rivets: Women at Work in World War II.* Her essay, "Memory Book," was a notable essay in *Best American Essays 2010.* She feels most at home walking along the Pacific Ocean and hiking in Desolation Wilderness.

RM Yager is a retired nurse/teacher/photographer whose topics are marginalized, at risk populations. Poetry is her vehicle to deliver words most people find unspeakable. She hopes to offer inclusion and wants to stop you in your tracks with controversial humor/tragedy within family and relationships, but she also loves whimsy, humor, and nature. She has been published in the US and internationally.

One of Bloomington's finest and most outspoken poets, **Hiromi Yoshida**'s chapbooks are *Icarus Burning, Epicanthus,* and *Icarus Redux.*

Her poems have been included in the INverse Poetry Archive and nominated for the Pushcart Prize, Best of the Net, the Wilder Poetry Book Prize, the New Women's Voices Poetry Prize, and the Gerald Cable Book Award. Her *LSPJ* Editor's Choice Award-winning poem, "Say Her Asian Name," will be included in her forthcoming poetry chapbook, *Icarus Superstar* (Alien Buddha Press, 2023).